1000

NINJA FOODI

COOKBOOK
FOR BEGINNERS AND ADVANCED USERS

Easy & Delicious Recipes to Air Fry, Pressure Cook, Dehydrate, and more

BY
Barbara Cutts

DISCLAIMER

The information contained in this book is geared for educational and entertainment purposes only. Strenuous efforts have been made towards providing accurate, up to date and reliable complete information. The information in this book is true and complete to the best of our knowledge. Neither the publisher nor the author takes any responsibility for any possible consequences of reading or enjoying the recipes in this book. The author and publisher disclaim any liability in connection with the use of information contained in this book. Under no circumstance will any legal responsibility or blame be apportioned against the author or publisher for any reparation, damages, or monetary loss due to the information herein, either directly or indirectly.

Table of Contents

Function Keys of Your Ninja Foodi:

Ninja Foodi comes with many buttons for optimum operation of the unit which includes steam, slow cook, pressure cook, sear/sauté button, air crisp, broil, bake /roast and keep warm, buttons respectively. It also has buttons for temperature and time controls, start/stop button. The buttons and their functions are shown below:

1. **Pressure Cook:**

This button helps you to cook your meal up to 4 hours using high or low pressure. As earlier said, it is possible to adjust the cooking time to 1-minute increment for 1 hour. When the time is up, you may increase the time to 5 minutes and begin to cook up to 4 hours. Hence you can make a whole lot of meals.

2. **Air Crisp:**

This function gives you an opportunity to adjust the temperature to either 300°F or 400°F and also adjust to increase the cooking time to 2 minutes for the highest cooking time of 1 hour. The air crisp button is used in cooking many dishes like chicken tenders, French fries etc. Pressure cooked food can be crisp using this button.

3. **Bake/Roast:**

This setting in the Ninja is good for making roasted meats and baked foods. For this function, the Ninja Foodi uses the air-frying lid. There is no problem if you set the cooking time to 1-minute increment for 1 hour. When the time is up, you may increase the time to 5 minutes and begin to cook up to 4 hours. After the hour mark, you can increase the time in five-minute increments and cook for up to four hours.

4. **Steam:**

It is possible to steam your veggies and other meals by putting the pressure lid on the Ninja Foodi with the sealing valve in the vent position.

5. **Slow cook:**

This button also makes use of the pressure lid with the sealing valve in the vent position. It is possible for you to slow cook low or slow cook high. The cooking time can also be adjusted to 15 minutes increment for up to 12 hours. It is advisable to use the slow cook mode when cooking meals like stews, soup or pot roasts.

6. **Sear/Sauté:**

This button on the Ninja Foodi does not make use of the lid. It only has a temperature setting of 5 different modes respectively. These includes: medium, medium-high, high, low or medium-low, setting. Foods can be browned after cooking or before cooking. The button can also be used to make different kinds of sauces, gravies. This button functions the same as you would sear or sauté using your stovetop.

Steps on How to Use Your Ninja Foodi:

This appliance is a very friendly and easy-to-use kitchen unit.

For Ninja Foodi pressure cooker:

1. Always put your foods in the inner pot of the Ninja Foodi or you put your food in the Air Fryer basket. This is basically good for meats.

2. Press the power on function.

3. Close lid in place. Do not put the one that is attached.

4. Set the top steam valve to seal position and press the pressure function.

5. Adjust the temperature to either high or low using the + or − buttons respectively.

6. Set the cooking time using the + or − buttons.

7. Press Start button.

8. The Ninja Foodi will take a little time to reach pressure and then will count the number of minutes until it reaches zero minute.

For Ninja Foodi Air Fryer:

1. Make use of the lid that is attached.

2. Place the Air Fryer cooking basket inside the Ninja Foodi inner pot.

3. Place your food inside the cooking basket.

4. Lock the attached lid and switch on the Ninja Foodi by pressing the button at the bottom.

5. Push the air crisp button.

6. Select the temperature you want to use by pressing the + and − buttons.

7. Set the cooking time by pressing the + and − buttons.

8. Select start button.

Useful Tips & Tricks for Using Your Ninja Foodi

It is pertinent to inquire to know how to properly use a new appliance you bought. Ninja Foodi come with 2 distinct lids. One is for the electric pressure cooker while the other one is for the Air Fryer lid. It is possible to use both lids in on food. Immediately the pressure cooker is done, remove the pressure cooker lid and put the Air Fryer lid. This helps to crisp your food. Every new kitchen appliance you get comes with an operational manual to guide you on the proper usage of the unit. Below are some few tips for the proper usage of your Ninja Foodi:

1. Whenever you want to spray cooking spray on the inner pot of your Ninja Foodi, do not use aerosol cooking spray.

2. Try to use the recommended amount of water or broth if you are using the pressure-cooking button. Wrong usage of water may not give you the desired result.

3. When you are not using your Ninja Foodi, unplug from any power source so as to avoid the appliance switch on by itself even when you did not press the power on button.

4. It is not advisable to use your Ninja Foodi on your stove top. This can easily damage the unit.

Ninja Foodi Troubleshooting Tips

Every electronic appliance sometimes has trouble shooting or shows a faulty message on the display. Below are some of the major trouble shooting or problems you could find on your Ninja Foodi.

1. My appliance is taking a long time to come to pressure. Why?

It is important to know how long it takes your Ninja Foodi to come to pressure. Base on a particular temperature you choose, cooking time may vary. Temperature of the cooking pot at the moment of cooking including the amount of ingredients also makes cooking time to vary. If the cooking time is taking a longer time than necessary, make sure your silicone ring is fully seated and flush against the lid, make sure the pressure lid is fully closed and set the pressure release valve to seal position.

2. Why is the cooking time counting slowly?

You have to make sure you set the time correctly. Check if you did not use hours instead of minutes. Note that the HH stands for hours while the MM stands for minutes on the display window respectively. You can increase or decrease the cooking time.

3. How do I know when the appliance is pressurizing?

When the appliance is building pressure, the rotating lights will display on the display window. When you are using steam or pressure mode, light will rotate on the display screen. It means the appliance is preheating. Immediately the preheating process finishes, the normal cooking time starts counting.

4. When I'm using the steam mode, my unit is bringing out a lot of steam.

During cooking, steam releasing on the pressure release valve is normal. It is advisable to allow the pressure release valve in the vent position for Steam, Slow Cook, and Sear or Sauté mode.

5. Why can't I take off the pressure lid?

The Ninja Foodi has to be depressurized before the pressure lid can be opened. This is one of the safety measures put by the manufacturer. In order to do a quick pressure release, set the pressure release valve to the vent position. Immediately the pressure is released completely, the lid will be ready to open.

6. Do I need to lose the pressure release valve?

The answer is yes. You have to loosen the pressure release valve. It helps to circulate pressure through some release of small amount of steam while cooking is done for the result to be excellent.

Ninja Foodi Frequently Asked Questions and Answers:

Question 1: Can I deep fry chicken with this appliance?

Answer: Yes, it is possible. You can cook a chicken in your Ninja Foodi. This is a new modern way of cooking that can tender your food and progress to crisping the food using hot air and give you a crispy result.

Question 2: Can I Take My Ninja Pot from the Refrigerator and Put directly in the appliance?

Answer: Yes, you can do it if your pot was in the refrigerator.

Question 3: Can the Pot enter under the Broiler or the Oven?

Answer: Yes. It is possible but you have to be extra careful while putting or taking the pot out from the Ninja Foodi. It is only the lid that you do not need to put under the oven or the broiler.

Question 4: Can the Baking or cooking pan enter under the oven?

Answer: Yes. It is very possible and good to put the cooking pan under the oven. You just need to be careful while inserting the pan.

Question 5: Can I use the buffet settings to cook?

Answer: NO. It is not advisable to do that because the buffet function is just to keep temperature that is above 140°F when the food has been cooked to 165°F.

Question 6: What is the meaning of One-pot Meal Cooking?

Answer: These are important family meal that could be ready within 30 minutes time. The one pot helps in a quick clean up.

Question 7: What differentiate model op301 from model op305?

Answer: Model OP305 has the Dehydrate button while model OP301 has no dehydrate button. That's the major difference.

Question 8: Can you can food with Ninja Foodi?

Answer: No, you will not be able to can food with this appliance. You can only do it if you have a pressure canner can.

Question 9: Why is the time beeper not beeping?

Answer: You can check the volume level.

Question 10: Can I put frozen pork loin in my Ninja Foodi?

Answer: Yes. It is possible to do that. Frozen foods can be cooked with this appliance.

Question 11: If the Ninja foodi displays water, what is the meaning?

Answer: It means that you need to put more water into the Ninja Foodi. If at a point of putting more water and the error still show up, contact the customer care on 877581-7375.

Question 12: Can meat and cheese vegetables be cooked with this appliance?

Answer: No. Ninja Foodi was not meant for canning of foods. So, it will not work for you.

Ninja Foodi Pressure Releasing Methods:

This process is ideal for stopping all cooking process in order to avoid the food getting burnt. Foods like corn or broccoli etc. are ideal for this pressure releasing. There are two types of pressure release namely: Quick and natural pressure release.

1. **How to do a Ninja Foodi Quick Release**

Immediately the cooking time is up, keep the venting knob on Venting Position to enable Ninja Foodi quickly release the pressure inside the pressure cooker. To release all the pressure, it normally takes some few minutes. Before you open the lid, wait until the valve drops.

2. **How to do a Ninja Foodi Natural Release**

Immediately the cooking time is up, you have to wait until the valve drops and the lid is opened. In order to make sure all the pressure is released before opening the lid, keep the venting knob on Venting Position. This particular pressure release technique normally takes about 10 – 25 minutes but it depends on the amount of food in your cooker. To do the 10 – 15 minutes pressure release, when the cooking time is up, wait 10 – 15 minutes before moving the Venting Knob from Sealing Position to Venting Position so as to enable the remaining pressure to be released. Do not fail to wait for the floating valve to drop before you open the lid.

CHAPTER 1 - BREAKFAST AND BRUNCH RECIPES
Stuffed Baked Potatoes

Preparation time: 15 minutes

Cook time: 20 minutes,

Overall time: 35 minutes

Serves: 2 to 4 people

Recipe Ingredients:
- ❖ 4 large baked potatoes
- ❖ 2 tablespoons of melted butter
- ❖ 1 teaspoon of salt
- ❖ 1 teaspoon of black pepper
- ❖ 1 cup of grated cheddar cheese
- ❖ 6 slices of cook crisp & chop bacon
- ❖ 4 large eggs
- ❖ 2 tablespoons of chives, chop

Cooking Instructions
1. Select bake function and heat cooker to 350°F. Then cut an opening in the top of the potatoes. With a spoon, scoop out most of the center.

2. Brush with melted butter and sprinkle with salt and pepper. Divide ¾ of the cheese evenly among the potatoes and top with ¾ of the bacon.

3. Crack one egg into each potato then top with remaining bacon, cheese and chives.

4. Place on the rack of the cooker and secure the tender-crisp lid and set the timer for 20 minutes.

5. Egg whites should be cooked completely but the yolk should still be soft.

6. Serve immediately.

Cranberry Lemon Quinoa

Preparation time: 6 minutes

Cooking time: 20 minutes

Overall time: 26 minutes

Serves: 3 to 6 people

Recipe Ingredients:
- ❖ 16 ounces of quinoa
- ❖ 4 ½ cups of water
- ❖ ½ cup of brown packed sugar
- ❖ 1 teaspoon of lemon extract
- ❖ ½ teaspoon of salt
- ❖ ½ cup of dried cranberries

Cooking Instructions:

1. Add all ingredients, except the cranberries, to the cooker and stir thoroughly to mix.

2. Secure the lid and select pressure cooking on high, then set timer for 20 minutes.

3. When timer goes off, use natural release for 10 minutes. Then use quick release and remove the lid. After that, stir in cranberries.

4. Serve immediately and enjoy.

Cheesecake French Toast

Preparation time: 11 minutes

Cooking time: 50 minutes

Overall time: 61 minutes

Serves: 3 to 6 people

Recipe Ingredients:
- ❖ Butter flavored cooking spray
- ❖ 4 eggs
- ❖ ½ cup of sugar
- ❖ 1 cup of milk
- ❖ 1 ½ teaspoons of vanilla, divided
- ❖ 1/8 teaspoon of salt
- ❖ ½ pound of challah bread (cut in 1-inch cubes)
- ❖ ½ cup of strawberries, chopped
- ❖ 2 ounces of cream cheese, soft
- ❖ ¼ cup of powdered sugar

Cooking Instructions

1. Start by selecting bake function and heat the cooker to 350°F, after that, spray a baking dish with cooking spray.

2. Then in a large bowl, whisk together eggs, sugar, milk, 1 teaspoon vanilla, and salt until its smooth.

3. Add bread and strawberries and fold until the bread is thoroughly coated with the egg mixture.

4. In another bowl, beat cream cheese, powdered sugar, and remaining vanilla until smooth.

5. Place half the bread mixture in the prepared baking dish and drop half the cheese mixture by teaspoons over bread then repeat.

6. Carefully place the dish into the cooker and secure the tender-crisp lid. Then Bake for about 45 to 50 minutes or until its golden brown and a toothpick inserted in center comes out clean.

7. Remove the dish and let cool for about 10 minutes before serving immediately.

Ham and Broccoli Frittata

Preparation time: 11 minutes

Cooking time: 30 minutes

Overall time: 41 minutes

Serves: 3 to 6 people

Recipe Ingredients:

- ❖ 1 tablespoon of butter, soft
- ❖ 1 cup of red seeded and sliced pepper,
- ❖ 1 cup of cubed ham
- ❖ 2 cups of broccoli florets
- ❖ 4 eggs
- ❖ 1 cup of half-n- half
- ❖ 1 cup of cheddar cheese, grated
- ❖ 1 teaspoon of salt
- ❖ 2 teaspoons of pepper
- ❖ 2 cups of water

Cooking Instructions

1. Use the soft butter to grease a 6x3-inch baking dish. Then place the peppers in an even layer on the bottom of the dish and top with ham then broccoli.

2. In a mixing bowl, whisk together eggs, half-n-half, salt, and pepper together.

3. Stir in cheese and pour mixture over ingredients in the baking dish and cover with foil.

4. Pour 2 cups water into the cooking pot and place the rack inside. Place the baking dish on the rack and secure the lid.

5. Then select pressure cooking on high and set the timer for 20 minutes. When the timer goes off, release pressure naturally for 10 minutes, then quick release.

6. After that, remove the baking dish and let it cool at least 5 minutes. With a sharp knife, loosen the sides of the frittata then invert onto serving plate. Serve immediately.

Pumpkin Pecan Oatmeal

Preparation time: 5 minutes

Cooking time: 8 minutes

Overall time: 13 minutes

Serves: 2 to 4 people

Recipe Ingredients:

- ❖ 1 cup of water
- ❖ 2 cups of old-fashioned oats
- ❖ 1 ¾ cup of milk
- ❖ ½ cup of pumpkin puree
- ❖ 1 teaspoon of pumpkin pie spice
- ❖ ¼ teaspoon of vanilla
- ❖ ½ cup of maple syrup
- ❖ 2 tablespoons of chopped pecans

Cooking Instructions:

1. Add water, oats, milk, pumpkin, spice, vanilla, and syrup to the cooking pot and stir thoroughly to combine.

2. Secure the lid and select pressure cooking on high, then set timer for 8 minutes.

3. When timer goes off, release pressure naturally for 5 minutes, then use quick release for remaining pressure.

4. Stir oatmeal then ladle into bowls and top with pecans.

5. Plate, serve immediately and enjoy.

Chili Cheese Quiche

Preparation time: 6 minutes

Cooking time: 30 minutes

Overall time: 36 minutes

Serves: 2 to 4 people

Recipe Ingredients:
- ❖ Nonstick cooking spray
- ❖ 4 eggs
- ❖ 1 cup of half-n- half
- ❖ 10 ounces of diced green chilies
- ❖ ½ teaspoon of salt
- ❖ ½ teaspoon of cumin
- ❖ 1 cup of grated Mexican blend cheese
- ❖ ¼ cup of chopped cilantro

Cooking Instructions

1. Start by spraying a 6-inch baking pan with cooking spray.

2. In a mixing bowl, beat eggs then stir in half-n-half, chilies, salt, cumin, and half the cheese.

3. Pour into prepared pan and cover with foil, add 2 cups water to the cooking pot and add the rack. Place the pan on the rack and secure the lid.

4. Select pressure cooking on high and set timer for 20 minutes. When timer goes off, release pressure naturally for 10 minutes, then use quick release.

5. Remove the foil and sprinkle remaining cheese over the top. Secure the tender-crisp lid and set temperature to 375°F.

6. Cook for another 3 to 5 minutes or until cheese is melted and starts to brown.

7. Serve garnished with cilantro and enjoy.

Blueberry Muffins

Preparation time: 6 minutes

Cooking time: 20 minutes

Overall time: 26 minutes

Serves: 6 to 12 people

Recipe Ingredients:

- ❖ 2 ½ cups of oats
- ❖ 1 ½ cups of unsweetened almond milk
- ❖ Nonstick cooking spray
- ❖ 1 egg, lightly beaten
- ❖ 1/3 cup of pure maple syrup
- ❖ 2 tablespoons of coconut oil, melted
- ❖ 1 teaspoon of vanilla
- ❖ 1 teaspoon of cinnamon
- ❖ 1 teaspoon of baking powder
- ❖ ¼ teaspoon of salt
- ❖ 1 teaspoon of lemon zest, grated
- ❖ 1 cup of fresh blueberries

Cooking Instructions

1. In a large bowl, combine oats and milk, then cover and refrigerate overnight. Select bake function and heat to 375°F. Spray 2 6-cup muffin tins with cooking spray.

2. Whisk remaining ingredients into the oat mixture, then spoon into muffin tins.

3. Place the rack in the cooking pot and place muffin tin on it; these will need to be baked in 2 batches.

4. Secure the tender crisp lid and bake 20 minutes or until tops are golden brown. Serve warm immediately.

Banana Custard Oatmeal

Preparation time: 10 minutes

Cooking time: 40 minutes

Overall time: 50 minutes

Serves: 3 to 6 people

Recipe Ingredients:
- ❖ Butter flavored cooking spray
- ❖ 1 2/3 cups of unsweetened vanilla almond milk
- ❖ 2 large mashed bananas
- ❖ 1 cup of sliced bananas
- ❖ 1 cup of steel cut oats
- ❖ 1/3 cup of maple syrup
- ❖ 1/3 cup of walnuts, chopped
- ❖ 2 beaten eggs
- ❖ 1 tablespoon of melted butter
- ❖ 1 ½ teaspoon of cinnamon
- ❖ 1 teaspoon of baking powder
- ❖ 1 teaspoon of vanilla extract
- ❖ ½ teaspoon of nutmeg
- ❖ ¼ teaspoon of salt
- ❖ 2 ½ cups of water

Cooking Instructions:
1. Spray a 1 ½ quart baking dish with cooking spray.

2. In a large bowl, combine all ingredients thoroughly and transfer to prepared baking dish.

3. Pour 1 ½ cups water into the cooking pot and add the trivet. Place dish on the trivet and secure the lid.

4. Select pressure cooking on high and set timer for 40 minutes.

5. When timer goes off, release pressure naturally for 10 minutes, then use quick release. Whisk oatmeal well then serve and enjoy.

Pumpkin Breakfast Bread

Preparation time: 11 minutes

Cooking time: 3 hours

Overall time: 3 hrs. 11 minutes

Serves: 14 people

Recipe Ingredients:

- ❖ 1 ½ teaspoon of baking soda
- ❖ 3 cups of pumpkin puree
- ❖ 1 teaspoon of vanilla extract
- ❖ 2 teaspoons of pumpkin pie spice
- ❖ Nonstick cooking spray
- ❖ 2 cups of whole wheat pastry flour
- ❖ ½ cup of coconut oil, melted
- ❖ ¾ cup of honey
- ❖ 2 eggs
- ❖ 1 mashed banana
- ❖ ½ cup of chopped & divided walnuts,

Cooking Instructions:

1. Start by spraying the cooking pot with cooking spray. Then in a large bowl, combine flour, baking soda, and pumpkin spice.

2. Make a **"well"** in the middle of the dry ingredients and add oil, honey, eggs, pumpkin, vanilla, and banana, and ¼ cup of the walnuts and mix well to thoroughly combine all ingredients.

3. Pour batter into cooking pot and sprinkle remaining walnuts over the top. Place two paper towels over the top of the pot and secure the lid.

4. Select slow cooking function on high and set timer for 2 hours. When timer goes off check bread, it should pass the toothpick test.

5. If it is not done, continue cooking for another 30 to 60 minutes. When bread is done, transfer to a wire rack to cool.

6. Serve immediately and enjoy.

Breakfast Pies

Preparation time: 10 minutes

Cooking time: 20 minutes

Overall time: 30 minutes

Serves: 2 to 4 people

Recipe Ingredients:
- ❖ 1 ½ cups of mozzarella cheese, grated
- ❖ 2/3 cup of almond flour, sifted
- ❖ 4 beaten eggs
- ❖ 4 tablespoons of butter
- ❖ 6 slices of cooked crisp & crumbled bacon

Cooking Instructions

1. Select air-fryer function and heat cooker to 400°F. In a microwave safe bowl, melt the mozzarella cheese until it's even then stir in flour until well combined.

2. Roll the dough out between 2 sheets of parchment paper, and then use a sharp knife to cut dough into 4 equal rectangles.

3. Heat the butter in a skillet over medium heat and add the eggs and scramble to desired doneness.

4. Divide eggs evenly between the four pieces of dough, placing them on one side; and then top with bacon.

5. Fold dough over filling and seal the edges with a fork. Poke a few holes on the top of the pies.

6. Place the pies in the fryer basket in a single layer. Secure the tender-crisp lid and bake for 20 minutes, turning over halfway through.

7. Serve immediately.

Peaches & Brown Sugar Oatmeal

Preparation time: 5 minutes

Cooking time: 8 hours

Overall time: 8 hrs. 6 minutes

Serves: 4 to 8 people

Recipe Ingredients:

- ❖ Nonstick cooking spray
- ❖ 2 cups of steel cut oats
- ❖ 8 cups of water
- ❖ 1 teaspoon of cinnamon
- ❖ ½ cup of brown sugar
- ❖ 1 teaspoon of vanilla
- ❖ 1 cup of cubed peaches

Cooking Instructions

1. Start by spraying the cooking pot with cooking spray.

2. Add the oats, water, cinnamon, sugar, and vanilla to the pot and stir thoroughly to combine.

3. Secure the lid and select slow cooker function on low then set timer for 8 hours.

4. Stir in peaches and serve immediately.

Spinach & Sausage Casserole

Preparation time: 10 minutes

Cooking time: 7 hours

Overall time: 17 minutes

Serves: 4 to 8 people

Recipe Ingredients:
- ❖ Nonstick cooking spray
- ❖ 1 pound of pork breakfast sausage
- ❖ 1 yellow diced onion
- ❖ 1 ½ teaspoons of oregano
- ❖ 5 cups of packed baby spinach
- ❖ 4 cups of diced potatoes
- ❖ 1 ¼ cups of grated swiss cheese
- ❖ ¼ cup of Parmesan cheese
- ❖ 8 eggs
- ❖ 2 cups of milk
- ❖ 2 teaspoons of Dijon mustard
- ❖ 1 ½ teaspoons of salt
- ❖ ¼ teaspoon of black pepper

Cooking Instructions:
1. Spray the cooking pot with cooking spray and select the sauté function on med-high.

2. Add the sausage, onion, and oregano and cook, stirring to break up the sausage until no longer pink for about 8 to 10 minutes.

3. Whisk in the spinach and cook for about 2 minutes or until wilted. Then set the cooker to the slow cooker function on low heat.

4. Add the potatoes, 1 cup of Swiss cheese, and the parmesan cheese and mix thoroughly well.

5. In a large bowl, whisk eggs, milk, mustard, salt, and pepper until smooth. After that, pour over ingredients in the cooking pot and stir to combine.

6. Secure the lid and set the timer for 6 hours. Casserole is done when the edges start to brown and the eggs are set. If it is not done, recover and cook for another 60 minutes or until it's done.

7. When the casserole is set, top with remaining cheese and cover. Cook just until the cheese melts for about 5 minutes.

Sausage & Egg Stuffed Peppers

Preparation time: 11 minutes

Cooking time: 6 hours

Overall time: 6 hrs. 11 minutes

Serves: 2 to 4 people

Recipe Ingredients:
- ½ pound of breakfast sausage
- 4 bell peppers
- ½ cup of water
- 6 eggs
- ½ cup of cheddar Jack cheese, grated
- 4 ounces of green chilies, diced
- ¼ teaspoon of salt
- 1/8 teaspoon of pepper
- 2 tablespoons of diced green onion,

Cooking Instructions
1. Set cooker to sauté on med-high heat. Then add sausage and cook, breaking up with spatula, until no longer pink. Transfer to a bowl and drain off the grease.

2. Cut the tops off the peppers and remove the seeds and ribs. Place in the cooking pot and pour the water around them.

3. In a medium bowl, whisk eggs until it is smooth. Stir in cheese, chilies, salt, and pepper until it is thoroughly combined; then fill the peppers with the egg mixture.

4. Secure the lid and set to slow cooker function on high and set the timer for 4 hours.

5. Casserole is done when the eggs are set, if not done when the timer goes off, cook for another 1 to 2 hours.

6. Garnish with green onions and serve.

Breakfast Souffles

Preparation time: 15 minutes

Cooking time: 20 minutes

Overall time: 35 minutes

Serves: 3 to 6 people

Recipe Ingredients:

- ❖ 1 pound of chopped thick cut bacon,
- ❖ 8 ounces of chopped pork sausage links
- ❖ Nonstick cooking spray
- ❖ 5 separated eggs
- ❖ 1/3 cup of heavy cream
- ❖ ½ cup of grated cheddar cheese,
- ❖ ½ teaspoon of salt
- ❖ ¼ teaspoon of thyme

Cooking Instructions

1. Set cooker to sauté function on medium-high. Then add the bacon and cook until it's almost crispy. Transfer to a paper towel lined plate.

2. Add the sausage and cook until done. Transfer to a separate paper towel lined plate.

3. Drain off fat and set cooker to air-fry setting and preheat to 350°F. Spray 6 ramekins with cooking spray. Then in a large bowl, beat egg whites until stiff peaks form.

4. In a medium bowl, whisk the yolks, cream, cheese, and seasonings together, stir in the meats and mix thoroughly well.

5. Gently fold the yolk mixture into the egg whites. Spoon the mixture into the prepared ramekins.

6. Place the rack in the cooker and place the ramekins on top. Secure the tender-crisp lid and bake for 20 minutes, or until the soufflés have puffed up. Serve immediately.

Cinnamon Crumb Donuts

Preparation time: 11 minutes

Cooking time: 10 minutes

Overall Time: 21 minutes

Serves: 3 to 6 people

Recipe Ingredients:

- ❖ 1 room temperature egg,
- ❖ ½ cup of stevia confectioners' sugar
- ❖ ½ tablespoon of milk
- ❖ ½ teaspoon of vanilla
- ❖ ¼ teaspoon of cinnamon
- ❖ ¼ cup of butter (cut in cubes)
- ❖ ½ cup of packed stevia brown sugar
- ❖ 2 ½ tablespoons of melted butter
- ❖ ½ teaspoon of salt
- ❖ 1 teaspoon of baking powder
- ❖ ½ cup of sour cream
- ❖ Butter flavored cooking spray
- ❖ ¼ cup of granulated stevia
- ❖ 1 cup + 3 ½ tablespoons of divided flour

Cooking Instructions:

1. Select air-fryer function and heat cooker to 350°F. Spray a 6 mold donut pan with cooking spray.

2. In a small bowl, combine ¼ cup granulated Stevia, 3 ½ tablespoons flour, and ¼ teaspoon cinnamon.

3. With a pastry cutter, or fork, cut in the cold butter until mixture resembles coarse crumbs. Cover and chill until ready to use.

4. In a large bowl, stir together 1 cup flour, the Stevia brown sugar, salt, and baking powder.

5. In a separate bowl, whisk together sour cream, melted butter, and egg. Stir into dry ingredients just until its combined. Then spoon dough into prepared pan.

6. Sprinkles chilled crumb topping evenly over the tops and place the pan in the cooker and secure the tender-crisp lid.

7. Cook for 10 to 11 minutes or donuts pass the toothpick test. Cool in the pan for 10 minutes then transfer to a wire rack.

8. In a small bowl, whisk together Stevia powdered sugar substitute, milk, and vanilla. Drizzle donuts with glaze and serve.

Sausage & Broccoli Frittata

Preparation time: 10 minutes

Cooking time: 25 minutes

Overall time: 35 minutes

Serves: 5 to 10 people

Recipe Ingredients:
- ❖ 1 tablespoon of olive oil
- ❖ 1 pound of country-style pork sausage
- ❖ 4 cups of broccoli florets
- ❖ 1 chopped onion
- ❖ ½ teaspoon of salt
- ❖ ¼ teaspoon of pepper
- ❖ 14 eggs
- ❖ ½ cup of milk
- ❖ 2 cups of grated cheddar cheese

Cooking Instructions:
1. Select sauté function on med-high heat. Then add olive oil, once it's hot, add sausage, broccoli, onions, salt, and pepper.

2. Cook, stirring frequently, until sausage is no longer pink, then drain the fat.

3. In a large bowl, whisk together eggs, milk, and cheese and pour over sausage mixture.

4. Set cooker to bake function on 350°F and secure the tender-crisp lid and set timer to 20 minutes.

5. Frittata is done when eggs are set. Let it cool about 5 to 10 minutes before serving.

6. Serve and enjoy immediately

Bacon & Egg Poppers

Preparation time: 10 minutes

Cooking time: 25 minutes

Overall time: 35 minutes

Serves: 3 to 6 people

Recipe Ingredients:
- ❖ 8 eggs
- ❖ Salt and pepper, to taste
- ❖ 12 slices of bacon
- ❖ 4 jalapeno peppers
- ❖ 3 ounces of soft cream cheese
- ❖ ½ teaspoon of garlic powder
- ❖ ½ teaspoon of onion powder
- ❖ Nonstick cooking spray
- ❖ ½ cup of cheddar cheese, grated

Cooking Instructions

1. Select air-fryer function and heat cooker to 375°F.

2. Heat a skillet over med-high heat and cook bacon until almost crisp but still pliable. Remove to paper towels to drain and reserve bacon fat for later.

3. Remove the seeds from 3 of the jalapenos and chop them. With the remaining jalapeno, slice into rings.

4. In a large bowl, beat together cream cheese, 1 tablespoon bacon fat, chopped jalapenos, eggs, and seasonings.

5. Spray 26-cup muffin tins with cooking spray and place one slice bacon around the edges of each cup.

6. Pour egg mixture into cups, filling ¾ full then top with cheddar cheese and a jalapeno ring.

7. Place muffin pan, one at a time, in the cooker, secure the tender-crisp lid and bake for 20 to 25 minutes or until eggs are cooked. Repeat with other pan and serve immediately.

Butternut Breakfast Squash

Preparation time: 10 minutes

Cooking time: 15 minutes

Overall time: 25 minutes

Serves: 2 to 4 people

Recipe Ingredients:
- ❖ 2 teaspoons of maple syrup
- ❖ 1 tablespoon of peanut butter
- ❖ 1 tablespoon of coconut oil
- ❖ 12 ounces of cubed butternut squash
- ❖ ¼ teaspoon of cinnamon
- ❖ ¼ teaspoon of all-spice

Cooking Instructions

1. Select sauté function on medium heat and add the coconut oil to the cooking pot.

2. Then add the squash and cook until it starts to soften, for about 8 to 10 minutes.

3. Add remaining ingredients and mix very well. Cook for about 2 to 3 minutes longer until its heated through.

4. Serve warm immediately.

Ham and Hash Brown Casserole

Preparation time: 15 minutes

Cooking time: 7 hours

Overall time: 7 hrs. 15 minutes

Serves: 6 to 12 people

Recipe Ingredients:

- ❖ Nonstick cooking spray
- ❖ 30 ounces of shredded & frozen hash browns
- ❖ 1-pound diced ham,
- ❖ 1 diced onion
- ❖ 1 diced red bell pepper
- ❖ 1 diced orange bell pepper
- ❖ 1 ½ cups of grated cheddar cheese
- ❖ 12 eggs
- ❖ 1 cup of milk
- ❖ 4 ounces of diced green chilies
- ❖ 1 tablespoon of dijon mustard
- ❖ ½ teaspoon of garlic powder
- ❖ ½ teaspoon of pepper
- ❖ ¼ teaspoon of salt

Cooking Instructions:

1. Start by spraying the cooking pot with cooking spray.

2. Layer half the hash browns, ham, onions, peppers, and cheese in the pot; repeat layers.

3. Then in a large bowl, whisk together the eggs, milk, green chilies, and seasonings until it's thoroughly combined; then pour over ingredients in the cooking pot.

4. Secure the lid and set to slow cooker function on low heat and set the timer for 7 hours. Casserole is done when the eggs are set.

5. Plate, serve and enjoy.

Cranberry Vanilla Oatmeal

Preparation time: 6 minutes

Cooking time: 8 hours

Overall time: 8 hrs. 6 minutes

Serves: 6 people

Recipe Ingredients:
- ❖ Nonstick cooking spray
- ❖ 1 ½ teaspoon of cinnamon
- ❖ 2 ½ tsp of vanilla
- ❖ 1 ½ cups of steel cut oats
- ❖ 4 ½ cups of water
- ❖ 1 ½ cups of dried cranberries

Cooking Instructions:

1. Start by spraying the cooking pot with cooking spray.

2. Then add the oats, water, cinnamon, and vanilla and stir thoroughly to combine.

3. Secure the lid and set to slow cooker on low heat, set timer for 8 hours. When timer goes off stir in cranberries.

4. Plate and serve.

Carrot Cake Muffins

Preparation time: 10 minutes

Cook time: 30 minutes

Overall time: 40 minutes

Serves: 6 to 12 people

Recipe Ingredients:
- ¾ cup of sifted almond flour
- ½ cup of coconut flour
- 1 teaspoon of baking soda
- ½ teaspoon of baking powder
- 1 teaspoon of cinnamon
- ¼ teaspoon of salt
- ¼ teaspoon of cloves
- ¼ teaspoon of nutmeg

- 2 eggs
- ½ cup of honey
- 1 teaspoon of vanilla
- ¼ cup of unsweetened coconut milk
- 2 tablespoons of melted coconut oil
- 1 mashed banana
- 1 ½ cups of grated carrots

Cooking Instructions:
1. Select the bake function and heat cooker to 350°F. Line 26-cup muffin tins with liners.

2. In a medium bowl, combine flours, baking soda, baking powder, cinnamon, salt, cloves, and nutmeg.

3. In a large bowl, beat eggs, honey, vanilla, and milk together until thoroughly combined.

4. Add the melted oil and mix well. Add the banana and beat to combine and stir in dry ingredients until it is mixed in, then fold in the carrots.

5. Spoon into prepared muffin tins about ¾ full.

6. Place muffin tin, one at a time on the rack in the cooker and secure the tender-crisp lid. Bake for 25 to 30 minutes, or until muffins pass the toothpick test. Serve and enjoy immediately.

Ham and Spinach Breakfast Bake

Preparation time: 10 minutes

Cooking time: 30 minutes

Overall time: 40 minutes

Serves: 3 to 6 people

Recipe Ingredients:
- ❖ Nonstick cooking spray
- ❖ 10 eggs
- ❖ 1 cup of chopped spinach
- ❖ 1 cup of chopped ham
- ❖ 1 cup of chopped red peppers
- ❖ 1 cup of chopped onion
- ❖ 1 teaspoon of garlic powder
- ❖ ½ teaspoon of onion powder
- ❖ ¼ teaspoon of salt
- ❖ ¼ teaspoon of pepper
- ❖ 1 cup of grated Swiss cheese

Cooking Instructions

1. Select the bake function and heat cooker to 350°F; then spray the cooking pot with cooking spray.

2. In a large bowl, whisk eggs together; add remaining ingredients and mix to combine well.

3. Pour into cooking pot and secure the tender-crisp lid. Cook for about 25 to 30 minutes, or until eggs are set and top has started to brown.

4. Let it cool for 5 minutes before serving. Plate, serve and enjoy.

Savory Oatmeal

Preparation time: 6 minutes

Cooking time: 10 minutes

Overall time: 16 minutes

Serves: 2 people

Recipe Ingredients:

- ❖ 2 cups of low sodium chicken broth
- ❖ ¾ cup of old-fashioned oats
- ❖ ¼ teaspoon of divided salt
- ❖ 1 tablespoon of olive oil
- ❖ 1 tablespoon of unsalted butter,
- ❖ 8 ounces of sliced baby bella mushrooms
- ❖ ¼ teaspoon of pepper
- ❖ 1 cup of fresh baby spinach
- ❖ 2 eggs
- ❖ ½ cup of halved cherry tomatoes

Cooking Instructions:

1. Add the broth, oats, and 1/8 teaspoon salt to the cooking pot, stir thoroughly to combine.

2. Secure the lid and select pressure cooking function on high and set timer to 5 minutes.

3. Heat oil and butter in a medium skillet over low heat until butter has melted.

4. Add mushrooms and season with salt and pepper. Cook for 4 to 5 minutes, or until mushrooms are tender.

5. Stir in spinach and cook until it wilts for about 2 minutes, then transfer to a plate.

6. In the same skillet, crack 2 eggs and fry them the way you like them. When the timer goes off, use quick release to remove the lid.

7. Stir the oatmeal and ladle into bowls. Top each bowl with spinach mixture, an egg, and tomatoes. Serve immediately.

Banana Coconut Loaf

Preparation time: 11 minutes

Cooking time: 35 minutes

Overall time: 46 minutes

Serves: 8 people

Recipe Ingredients:
- ❖ Nonstick cooking spray
- ❖ 1 ¼ cup of whole wheat flour
- ❖ ½ cup of coconut flakes, unsweetened
- ❖ 2 teaspoons of baking powder
- ❖ ½ teaspoons of baking soda
- ❖ ½ teaspoons of salt
- ❖ 1 cup of mashed banana,
- ❖ ¼ cup of melted coconut oil
- ❖ 2 tablespoons of honey

Cooking Instructions

1. Select the bake function on heat cooker to 350°F. Spray an 8-inch loaf pan with cooking spray.

2. In a large bowl, combine flour, coconut, baking powder, baking soda, and salt.

3. In a separate bowl, combine banana, oil, and honey. Add to dry ingredients and mix well and spread batter in prepared pan.

4. Secure the tender-crisp lid and bake 30 to 35 minutes or until loaf passes the toothpick test.

5. Remove pan from the cooker and let cool 10 minutes. Invert loaf to a wire rack and cool completely before slicing. Serve immediately.

Chocolate Banana Muffins

Preparation time: 10 minutes

Cooking time: 25 minutes

Overall time: 35 minutes

Serves: 12 people

Recipe Ingredients:

- ❖ 1 cup of sifted almond flour
- ❖ ½ teaspoon of baking powder
- ❖ 1/8 teaspoon of salt
- ❖ 2 eggs
- ❖ ¼ cup of Stevia
- ❖ ½ teaspoon of almond extract
- ❖ 3 mashed bananas
- ❖ 2 tablespoons of unsweetened cocoa powder
- ❖ 1 tablespoon of sliced almonds

Cooking Instructions

1. Select bake function and heat cooker to 325°F. Line 2 6-cup of muffin tins with liners.

2. In a large bowl, combine flour, baking powder, and salt. Then add remaining ingredients, except almonds, and beat until thoroughly combined.

3. Spoon into liners and top with sliced almonds. Place muffin tin, one at a time, in the cooker and secure the tender-crisp lid.

4. Bake for about 25 to 30 minutes or until muffins pass the toothpick test. Serve warm and enjoy.

CHAPTER 2 - FISH AND SEAFOOD RECIPES
Arroz Con Cod

Preparation time: 11 minutes

Cooking time: 30 minutes

Overall time: 41 minutes

Serves: 2 to 4 people
Recipe Ingredients:
- ¼ cup of olive oil
- 2 tablespoons of chopped garlic
- ½ cup of chopped red onion
- ½ cup of chopped red bell pepper
- ½ cup of green bell pepper, chopped
- 2 cups of long grain rice
- 3 tablespoons of tomato paste
- 2 teaspoons of turmeric
- 2 tablespoons of cumin
- ½ teaspoon of salt
- ¼ teaspoon of pepper
- 4 cups of chicken broth
- 1 bay leaf
- 1 pound cod (cut in bite-size pieces)
- ½ cup of cooked peas
- 4 tablespoons of chopped pimento
- 4 teaspoons of chopped cilantro

Cooking Instructions:

1. Add the oil to the cooking pot and set to sauté on med-high. Then add the garlic, onion, and peppers, and cook, stirring frequently for 2 minutes.

2. Stir in rice, tomato paste, and seasonings, and cook for another 2 minutes.

3. Add the broth and bay leaf and bring to a boil; then reduce heat, cover, and let simmer for 5 minutes.

4. Add the fish, recover the pot and cook about 15 to 20 minutes until all the liquid is absorbed. Turn off the cooker and let sit for 5 minutes.

5. Spoon onto plates and top with cooked peas, pimento and cilantro. Then serve immediately.

Crab Cakes with Spicy Dipping Sauce

Preparation time: 6 minutes

Cooking time: 20 minutes

Overall time: 26 minutes

Serves: 2 to 4 people

Recipe Ingredients:
- ❖ 1/3 cup + ¼ cup of mayonnaise (divided)
- ❖ 1 teaspoon of hot sauce
- ❖ Nonstick cooking spray
- ❖ ¼ cup of bread crumbs
- ❖ ¼ cup + 1 tablespoon of finely chopped celery (divided)
- ❖ 4 teaspoons of Cajun seasoning (divided)
- ❖ 2 tablespoons of chopped fresh parsley (divided)
- ❖ 8 ounces of jumbo lump crab meat
- ❖ ¼ cup of finely chopped green bell pepper
- ❖ ¼ cup + 1 tablespoon of finely chopped red bell pepper (divided)
- ❖ 2 tablespoons of finely chopped green onions
- ❖ 1 tablespoon + 2 teaspoon of spicy brown mustard (divided)

Cooking Instructions:

1. Start by spraying the fryer basket with cooking spray.

2. Then in a small bowl, combine 1/3 cup mayonnaise, 2 teaspoons mustard, hot sauce, 1 tablespoon celery, 1 tablespoon red bell pepper, 2 teaspoons Cajun seasoning, and 1 tablespoon parsley and mix well.

3. Cover and refrigerate until it is ready to use. In a large bowl, combine all remaining ingredients with the crab, green bell pepper, onions, and bread crumbs and mix up well.

4. Form into 8 patties. Then place the patties in the fryer basket and add the tender-crisp lid, set to air-fry on 400°F.

5. Cook for 20 minutes, or until it turns golden brown, turning over halfway through cooking time. Serve with prepared sauce for dipping. Enjoy!

Shrimp and Sausage Gumbo

Preparation time: 16 minutes
Cooking time: 1 hr. 30 minutes
Overall time: 1 hr. 46 minutes
Serves: 4 to 8 people

Recipe Ingredients:

- ½ cup of peanut oil
- ½ cup of flour
- 1 green chopped bell pepper
- 1 chopped onion
- 3 stalks of chopped celery
- 4 chopped finely garlic cloves
- 1 tablespoon of cajun seasoning
- 1 low sodium quart chicken broth
- 1 cup of water
- 2 teaspoons of worcestershire sauce
- ¼ teaspoon of pepper
- ½ teaspoon of salt
- 12 ounces smoked and ouille sausage sliced ¼-inch thick
- 2 pounds of peeled and deveined shrimp
- 3 green chopped onions
- Hot sauce to taste

Cooking Instructions:

1. Add the oil to the cooking pot and set to sauté on medium heat. Then whisk in the flour until it is smooth.

2. Cook, while stirring until roux turns golden brown. Reduce heat to med-low and cook for about 20 to 30 minutes until roux is a deep brown.

3. Add the bell pepper, onion, and celery and increase heat to med-high. Cook, stirring frequently about 5 minutes. Add the garlic and cook 2 minutes more and stir in Cajun seasoning.

4. Stirring constantly, slowly add the broth and water. Bring to a simmer and add the Worcestershire, pepper, and salt.

5. Reduce heat to medium and simmer 30 minutes. Add the sausage and cook until it is heated through for about 5 minutes.

6. Add the shrimp and cook until they turn pink for about 5 minutes. Serve garnished with green onions and hot sauce to taste over cooked rice.

Indian Cod and Basmati Rice

Preparation time: 21 minutes

Cooking time: 30 minutes

Overall time: 51 minutes

Serves: 4 to 8 people

Recipe Ingredients:

- ❖ 1 ½ teaspoons of turmeric (divided)
- ❖ 2 teaspoons of chili powder
- ❖ 1 ¼ teaspoons of salt (divided)
- ❖ 2 pounds of cod (cut in large pieces)
- ❖ 3 tablespoons of butter
- ❖ 1 chopped onion
- ❖ 1 teaspoon of grated ginger
- ❖ 4 bay leaves
- ❖ 1 cinnamon stick
- ❖ 5 whole cloves
- ❖ 5 cardamom pods
- ❖ 1 teaspoon of ground coriander
- ❖ 1 teaspoon of garam masala
- ❖ 2 cups of water
- ❖ 1 cup of unsweetened coconut milk
- ❖ 3 seeded and chopped Roma tomatoes,
- ❖ 4 tablespoons of chopped cilantro (divided)
- ❖ 1 tablespoon of fresh mint, chopped
- ❖ 3 cups brown basmati rice, rinsed & drained

Cooking Instructions:

1. Combine ½ teaspoon of turmeric, chili powder, and ¼ teaspoon of salt in a small bowl and sprinkle over fish; then let it sit for 20 minutes.

2. Add the butter to the cooking pot and set to sauté on medium heat, add onion and cook until it is soft.

3. Add ginger along with all the remaining spices and cook for about 1 to 2 minutes until fragrant.

4. Add the fish and cook, stirring gently, until it is cooked through for about 2 to 3 minutes. Then transfer fish to a plate and turn off the sauté mode.

5. Add the water and coconut milk, and stir, scraping up any brown bits from the bottom of the pot. Add tomatoes, 3 tablespoons of cilantro, and mint, and then stir to mix.

6. Sprinkle the rice on top and stir gently to make sure it is covered with liquid. Add the lid and set to pressure cook on high. Set the timer for 20 minutes.

7. When the timer goes off, use natural release to remove the lid. All of the liquid should be absorbed, if not, cook another 5 minutes.

8. To serve, fluff the rice and discard whole spices, spoon onto plates, top with fish and chopped cilantro.

9. Serve immediately.

Curried Salmon and Sweet Potatoes

Preparation time: 10 minutes

Cooking time: 20 minutes

Overall time: 30 minutes

Serves: 2 to 4 people

Recipe Ingredients:

- ❖ Nonstick cooking spray
- ❖ 2 peeled and cubed sweet potatoes
- ❖ 1 tablespoon+ 1 teaspoon of olive oil (divided)
- ❖ ½ teaspoon of salt
- ❖ 1 teaspoon of thyme
- ❖ 1 teaspoon of curry powder
- ❖ 1 teaspoon of honey
- ❖ ½ teaspoon of lime zest
- ❖ 1/8 teaspoon of crushed red pepper flakes
- ❖ 4 salmon filets

Cooking Instructions

1. Start by spraying the cooking pot with cooking spray.

2. In a large bowl, combine potatoes, 1 tablespoon oil, salt, and thyme and toss to coat the potatoes, then place in the cooking pot.

3. Add the tender-crisp lid and set to roast on 400°F and cook potatoes for 10 minutes.

4. In a small bowl, whisk together remaining oil, curry powder, honey, zest, and pepper flakes. Lay the salmon on a sheet of foil and brush the curry mixture over the top.

5. Open the lid and stir the potatoes and add the rack to the cooking pot and place the salmon, with the foil, on the rack.

6. Close the lid and continue to cook another 10 to 15 minutes until potatoes are tender and fish flakes easily with a fork. Serve immediately.

Sweet and Spicy Shrimp Bowls

Preparation time: 15 minutes

Cooking time: 5 minutes

Overall time: 20 minutes

Serves: 4 to 8 people

Recipe Ingredients:

- ❖ ½ cup of chopped green onions
- ❖ 1 seeded and chopped jalapeno pepper
- ❖ 1 teaspoon of red chili flakes
- ❖ 8 ounces of drained crushed pineapple
- ❖ 2 tablespoons of honey
- ❖ 1 zested and juiced lime
- ❖ 1 tablespoon of olive oil
- ❖ 2 pounds of large shrimp (peeled & deveined)
- ❖ ¼ teaspoon of salt
- ❖ 2 cups of cooked brown rice

Cooking Instructions:

1. Combine green onions, jalapeno, chili flakes, pineapple, honey, lime juice, and zest in a small bowl and mix thoroughly well.

2. Add the oil to the cooking pot and set to saute on medium heat. Sprinkle the shrimp with salt and cook for 3 to 5 minutes or until they turn pink.

3. Add the shrimp to the pineapple mixture and stir very well to coat. After that, spoon rice into bowls and top with shrimp mixture.

4. Serve immediately and enjoy.

Clam and Corn Chowder

Preparation time: 5 minutes

Cooking time: 5 hrs.

Overall time: 5 hrs. 5 minutes

Serves: 2 to 4 people

Recipe Ingredients:

- ❖ 1 cup of chicken broth, fat free
- ❖ 2 cups of peeled and cubed potatoes
- ❖ 1 cup of corn
- ❖ 1 peeled and chopped onion
- ❖ 1 bay leaf
- ❖ ½ teaspoon of marjoram
- ❖ ½ teaspoon of salt
- ❖ ¼ teaspoon of pepper
- ❖ 1 cup of skim milk
- ❖ 10½ ounces undrained minced clams,
- ❖ 2 teaspoons of cornstarch

Cooking Instructions:

1. Add the chicken broth, potatoes, corn, onion, bay leaf, marjoram, salt and pepper to the cooking pot, stir to mix.

2. Add the lid and set to slow cooking on high and cook for 4 to 5 hours or until potatoes are tender then discard the bay leaf.

3. Transfer the mixture to a food processor and pulse until it is smooth, after that, return to the cooking pot.

4. Stir in ¾ cup of milk and clams; cover and cook for another 15 minutes.

5. In a glass measuring cup, whisk together remaining milk and cornstarch until its smooth. Stir into chowder and cook, stirring 2 to 3 minutes or until its thickened.

6. Serve immediately.

Flounder Veggie Soup

Preparation time: 10 minutes

Cooking time: 20 minutes

Overall time: 30 minutes

Serves: 5 to 10 people

Recipe Ingredients:

- ❖ 2 cups of water (divided)
- ❖ 14 ounces of low sodium chicken broth
- ❖ 2 peeled and cubed pounds potatoes,
- ❖ 1 chopped onion
- ❖ 2 chopped stalks celery
- ❖ 1 chopped carrot
- ❖ 1 bay leaf
- ❖ 2 (12 ounces) cans evaporated milk, (fat free)
- ❖ 4 tablespoons of butter
- ❖ 1 pound of flounder filets (cut in 1/2-inch pieces)
- ❖ ½ teaspoon of thyme
- ❖ ¼ teaspoon of salt
- ❖ ¼ teaspoon of pepper

Cooking Instructions:

1. Start by adding 1 ½ cups of water, broth, potatoes, onion, celery, carrot, and the bay leaf to the cooking pot, then stir thoroughly to mix.

2. Add the lid and set to pressure cooker on high; set the timer for 8 minutes. When the timer goes off, use quick release to remove the lid.

3. Set cooker to sauté on med-low; stir in milk, butter, fish, thyme, salt and pepper and bring to a boil.

4. Then in a small bowl, whisk together remaining water and cornstarch until it is smooth.

5. Add to the soup and cook while stirring, until it is thickened. Discard the bay leaf and serve immediately.

Caramelized Salmon

Preparation time: 6 minutes
Cooking time: 10 minutes
Overall time: 16 minutes
Serves: 2 to 4 people

Recipe Ingredients:
- ❖ 1 tablespoon of melted coconut oil
- ❖ 1/3 cup of packed stevia brown sugar
- ❖ 3 tablespoons of fish sauce
- ❖ 1 ½ tablespoons of soy sauce
- ❖ 1 teaspoon of peeled and grated fresh ginger
- ❖ 2 teaspoons of finely grated lime zest
- ❖ 1 tablespoon of fresh lime juice
- ❖ ½ teaspoon of pepper
- ❖ 4 salmon fillets
- ❖ 1 tablespoon of sliced green onions
- ❖ 1 tablespoon of chopped cilantro

Cooking Instructions

1. Add the oil, brown sugar, fish sauce, zest, soy sauce, ginger, juice, and pepper to the cooking pot and stir thoroughly to mix.

2. Set to sauté on medium heat and bring mixture to a simmer, stirring frequently, and then turn heat off.

3. Add the fish to the sauce making sure it is covered; add the lid and set to pressure cooking on low then set the timer for 1 minute.

4. When the timer goes off let the pressure release naturally for about 5 minutes, the release is manually. Fish should be done when it flakes with a fork; transfer fish to a serving dish with the caramelized side up.

5. Set cooker back to sauté on medium and cook sauce for about 3 to 4 minutes or until it's thickened.

6. Spoon over fish and garnish with chopped green onions and scallions. Serve immediately and enjoy.

Classic Crab Imperial

Preparation time: 6 minutes

Cooking time: 25 minutes

Overall time: 31 minutes

Serves: 3 to 6 people

Recipe Ingredients:

- ❖ 1 cup of mayonnaise
- ❖ 2 eggs of lightly beaten
- ❖ 2 teaspoons of sugar
- ❖ 2 teaspoons of old bay seasoning
- ❖ 1 teaspoon of lemon juice
- ❖ 2 teaspoons of finely chopped parsley
- ❖ Pound of jumbo lump crab meat

Cooking Instructions:

1. In a medium bowl, combine mayonnaise, eggs, sugar, Old Bay, lemon juice, and parsley and mix thoroughly well.

2. Gently fold in crab and divide evenly between 6 ramekins and place in the cooking pot.

3. Add the tender-crisp lid and set to bake on 350°F, and then bake for about 20 to 25 minutes until the top is golden brown.

4. Let cool slightly before serving. Delicious!

Shrimp and Asparagus Risotto

Preparation time: 11 minutes
Cooking time: 10 minutes
Overall time: 21 minutes
Serves: 2 to 4 people

Recipe Ingredients:

- ❖ 1 tablespoon of butter
- ❖ ½ finely chopped onion
- ❖ 1 finely chopped garlic clove
- ❖ 1 cup of arborio rice
- ❖ 5 cups of water (divided)
- ❖ 1 cup of clam juice
- ❖ 1 tablespoon of olive oil
- ❖ ½ pound of small shrimp (peeled & deveined)
- ❖ ½ bunch asparagus (cut in 1-inch pieces)
- ❖ ¼ cup of parmesan cheese

Cooking Instructions:

1. Add butter to cooking pot and set to sauté on medium heat. Once butter melts, add onion and garlic and cook for about 5 minutes, stirring frequently.

2. Add the rice and stir to coat with butter mixture then transfer mixture to a 1-quart baking dish. Pour 1 cup of water and clam juice over rice mixture and cover tightly with foil.

3. Pour 2 cups of water in the cooking pot and add the rack. Place the rice mixture on the rack, secure the lid and set to pressure cooking on high then set timer for 10 minutes.

4. When timer goes off release the pressure quickly and remove the baking dish carefully and drain out any remaining water.

5. Set the cooker back to sauté on med-high and heat the oil. Add the shrimp and asparagus and cook, stirring, just until shrimp start to turn pink.

6. Add the shrimp and asparagus to the rice and stir to mix well. Recover tightly with foil. Pour 2 cups water back in the pot and add the rack.

7. Place the rice mixture back on the rack and secure the lid. Set to pressure cooking on high and set the timer for 4 minutes.

8. When the timer goes off, release the pressure quickly, remove the foil and stir. Serve immediately sprinkled with parmesan cheese.

Chili Mint Steamed Snapper

Preparation time: 6 minutes

Cooking time: 20 minutes

Overall time: 26 minutes

Serves: 2 to 4 people

Recipe Ingredients

- ❖ 2 pounds of whole snapper
- ❖ 2 tablespoons of white wine
- ❖ 2 tablespoons of soy sauce
- ❖ ¼ cup of peanut oil
- ❖ 2 teaspoons of ginger (cut in fine matchsticks)
- ❖ 2 sliced red chilies
- ❖ 1 cup of chopped fresh mint

Cooking Instructions:

1. Pour water in the cooking pot and add the rack.

2. Place the fish in a baking pan and add to the cooker and add the lid and set to steam for 15 minutes.

3. Transfer fish carefully to serving plate and pour out any remaining water in the pot.

4. Add the wine and soy sauce to the pot and set to sauté on medium heat. Cook until hot but not boiling and pour over fish.

5. Add the oil and let it get hot, after that, add the ginger and cook for about 1 minute or until its crisp.

6. Turn off the heat and the chilies. Pour this mixture over the fish and sprinkle with mint. Serve immediately.

Sweet and Spicy Shrimp

Preparation time: 11 minutes

Cooking time: 5 minutes

Overall time: 16 minutes

Serves: 2 to 4 people

Recipe Ingredients:

- ❖ ¾ cup of unsweetened pineapple juice,
- ❖ 1 sliced red bell pepper
- ❖ 1 ½ cups of grated cauliflower
- ❖ ¼ cup of dry white wine
- ❖ ½ cup of water
- ❖ 2 tablespoons of soy sauce
- ❖ 2 tablespoons of thai sweet chili sauce
- ❖ 1 tablespoon of chili paste
- ❖ 1-pound large shrimp, frozen
- ❖ 4 green onions chopped white and green separated
- ❖ 1 ½ cups of pineapple chunks (drained)

Cooking Instructions:

1. Add ¾ cup of pineapple juice along with remaining ingredients, except the pineapple chunks and green parts of the onion, to the cooking pot and stir to mix.

2. Add the lid and set to pressure cook on high, then set timer for 2 minutes. When the timer goes off, release pressure for 10 minutes before opening the pot.

3. Add the green parts of the onions and pineapple chunks and stir very well.

4. Serve immediately and enjoy.

Low Country Boil

Preparation time: 15 minutes

Cooking time: 10 minutes

Overall time: 25 minutes

Serves: 2 to 6 people

Recipe Ingredients:

- ❖ 1 pound of halved red potatoes
- ❖ 2 to 3 ears of corn (cut in thirds)
- ❖ 3 cups of water (divided)
- ❖ 2 tablespoons of old bay seasoning (divided)
- ❖ ½ teaspoon of salt
- ❖ 1 pound of andouille sausage (cut in 2-inch pieces)
- ❖ 1 ½ pounds of large shrimp (deveined, in shell)

Cooking Instructions:

1. Place the potatoes, corn, 2 cups of water, and half the seasonings in the cooking pot.

2. Add the lid and set to pressure cook on high, then set timer for 5 minutes. When timer goes off, use quick release to remove the lid.

3. Add the sausage, shrimp, remaining cup of water and remaining seasonings.

4. Add the lid and pressure cook on high for about 2 to 4 minutes, depending on how large your shrimps are.

5. Use quick release again to remove the lid. Scoop into large bowl, or plates, and sprinkle with more seasoning if desired.

6. Serve immediately.

Spanish Steamed Clams

Preparation time: 6 minutes

Cooking time: 20 minutes

Overall time: 26 minutes

Serves: 3 to 6 people

Recipe Ingredients:

- ❖ 3 tablespoons of olive oil
- ❖ 1 chopped fine onion
- ❖ 3 ounces of chopped prosciutto
- ❖ ¼ cup of dry sherry
- ❖ 36 littleneck clams

Cooking Instructions:

1. Add the oil to the cooking pot and set to sauté on med-high heat.

2. Add the onion and cook while stirring for 1 minutes, then reduce heat to low, add the lid and cook for about 10 to 15 minutes or until onion is soft.

3. Stir in remaining ingredients and increase heat to medium. Add the lid and cook for 5 minutes, or until the clams open.

4. Discard any unopened clams and serve immediately. Enjoy your meal!

Stuffed Cod

Preparation time: 11 minutes

Cooking time: 40 minutes

Overall time: 51 minutes

Serves: 2 to 4 people

Recipe Ingredients:
- ½ cup of bread crumbs
- 2 ½ teaspoons of garlic powder (divided)
- 1 ½ teaspoons of onion powder (divided)
- 1 tablespoons of parsley
- ¼ cup of parmesan cheese
- ½ teaspoon of salt
- ½ pound of rinsed and dried scallops
- 7 tablespoons of butter (divided)
- ½ pound of peeled and deveined shrimp
- 1 tablespoon of flour
- ¾ cup of low sodium chicken broth,
- ½ teaspoon of dill
- ½ cup of sour cream
- ½ tablespoon of lemon juice
- 4 patted dry cod filets

Cooking Instructions:

1. Set cooker to bake on 400°F, then place the rack in the cooking pot.

2. In a small bowl, combine bread crumbs, 2 teaspoons garlic powder, 1 teaspoon onion powder, parsley, parmesan cheese, and salt, mix thoroughly well.

3. Place the scallops in a baking pan and pour 3 tablespoons of melted butter over top.

4. Add the bread crumb mixture, and with a spatula mix together so scallops are coated on all sides.

5. Cover with foil and place in the cooking pot, then add the tender-crisp lid and bake for 10 minutes.

6. Uncover and add the shrimp and 3 tablespoons of butter to the scallops, use the spatula again to coat the shrimp.

7. Recover the dish and bake for another 10 minutes, then remove from cooking pot and uncover to cool.

8. In a small saucepan over medium heat, melt the remaining tablespoon of butter and add the flour and cook, whisking for 1 minute.

9. Whisk in broth, remaining garlic and onion powder, and dill until it's combined.

10. Bring mixture just to boil, whisking constantly, and cook for about 5 minutes until it's thickened.

11. Remove from heat let cool 5 minutes before stirring in sour cream and lemon juice.

12. Pour the scallop mixture onto a cutting board and chop. Add it back to the baking dish.

13. Spoon stuffing mixture onto the wide end of the fish filets and fold in half. Secure with a toothpick and place on a small baking sheet.

14. Spoon a small amount of the sauce over fish and place on the rack in the cooking pot.

15. Set to bake on 375°F, add the tender-crisp lid and cook 20 minutes. Transfer to serving plates and top with more sauce.

16. Serve immediately.

Tuna Zoodle Bake

Preparation time: 11 minutes

Cooking time: 20 minutes

Overall time: 31 minutes

Serves: 2 to 4 people

Recipe Ingredients:

- ❖ Nonstick cooking spray
- ❖ 2 zucchini (cut in noodles with a spiralizer)
- ❖ 1 teaspoon of olive oil
- ❖ ¼ cup of finely chopped onion,
- ❖ 6 ounces of drained tuna
- ❖ ½ tablespoon of tomato paste
- ❖ ½ cup of diced & drained tomatoes
- ❖ ¼ cup of skim milk
- ❖ ½ teaspoon of thyme
- ❖ ¼ teaspoon of salt
- ❖ ¼ teaspoon of pepper
- ❖ 1/8 cup of fat free parmesan cheese,
- ❖ 1/4 cup of grated cheddar cheese reduced fat

Cooking Instructions:

1. Start by spraying an 8 x 8-inch baking pan with cooking spray. After that, place the zucchini in an even layer in the prepared pan.

2. Add the oil to the cooking pot and set to sauté on med-high heat. Once the oil is hot, add the onion and cook for 2 minutes, or until its soft.

3. Stir in the tuna and tomato paste and cook for 1 minute more. Add the tomatoes, milk, thyme, salt, and pepper and bring to a low simmer.

4. Stir in parmesan cheese and cook until its melts. After that, pour the tuna mixture over the zucchini and sprinkle cheddar cheese over the top.

5. Wipe out the pat and place the baking pan in it. Add the tender-crisp lid and set to bake on 400°F. Bake for 15 minutes or until cheese is melted and bubbly. Serve immediately.

Shrimp Egg Rolls

Preparation time: 20 minutes

Cooking time: 10 minutes

Overall time: 30 minutes

Serves: 2 to 4 people

Recipe Ingredients:

- ❖ Nonstick cooking spray
- ❖ ¼ cup of soy sauce, low sodium
- ❖ 2 tablespoons of brown sugar
- ❖ 1 teaspoon of grated ginger
- ❖ 1 teaspoon of garlic powder
- ❖ 5 cups of coleslaw mix
- ❖ 2 sliced thin green onions
- ❖ 3 tablespoons of chopped cilantro
- ❖ 1 cup of chopped small shrimp
- ❖ 10 egg roll wrappers

Cooking Instructions:

1. Start by spraying the fryer basket with cooking spray.

2. Then in a small mixing bowl, whisk together, brown sugar, soy sauce, ginger, and garlic powder until it is thoroughly combined.

3. In a large bowl, combine coleslaw, green onions, cilantro, and shrimp and mix well.

4. Pour the soy sauce over the coleslaw and toss well to coat; let it sit for 15 minutes.

5. After 15 minutes, place in a colander and squeeze to remove as much liquid as possible.

6. Place egg roll wrappers on a work surface. Spoon about 1/3 cup of shrimp mixture in the center of each wrapper.

7. Fold opposite sides over filling, then one corner and roll up egg roll fashion. Place seam side down in fryer basket and spray lightly with cooking spray.

8. Add the tender-crisp lid and set to air-fry on 425°F. Cook for about 8 to 10 minutes or until it is golden brown and crisp, turning over halfway through cooking time. Once done, serve and enjoy.

Salmon Chowder

Preparation time: 20 minutes

Cooking time: 30 minutes

Overall time: 50 minutes

Serves: 4 to 8 people

Recipe Ingredients:
- ❖ 3 tablespoons of butter
- ❖ ½ cup of chopped celery
- ❖ ½ cup of chopped onion
- ❖ ½ cup of chopped green bell pepper
- ❖ 1 finely chopped clove garlic
- ❖ 14 ½ ounces of low sodium chicken broth
- ❖ 1 cup of peeled & cubed potatoes
- ❖ 1 cup of chopped carrots
- ❖ 1 teaspoon of salt
- ❖ ½ teaspoon of pepper
- ❖ 1 teaspoon of fresh dill, chopped
- ❖ 1 can cream-style corn
- ❖ 2 cups of half and half
- ❖ 2 cups of salmon, (cut in 1-inch pieces)

Cooking Instructions:

1. Add the butter to the cooking pot and set to sauté on med-high heat.

2. Add the celery, onion, green pepper, and garlic and cook, stirring frequently, until vegetables start to soften. Add the broth, potatoes, carrots, salt, pepper and dill and stir to mix.

3. Add the lid and set to pressure cook on high, then set the timer for 10 minutes. When the timer goes off, release the pressure with quick release.

4. Set back to sauté on medium and add the corn, cream, and salmon. Bring to a simmer and cook for 15 minutes, or until salmon is cooked through.

5. Serve immediately.

Blackened Salmon

Preparation time: 6 minutes

Cooking time: 10 minutes

Overall time: 16 minutes

Serves: 2 to 4 people

Recipe Ingredients:

- ❖ 1 tablespoon of plus 1 teaspoon of sweet paprika
- ❖ 1 teaspoon of garlic powder
- ❖ 1 teaspoon of oregano
- ❖ 1 teaspoon of salt
- ❖ ¾ teaspoon of cayenne pepper
- ❖ 2 tablespoons of olive oil
- ❖ 4 skin on salmon filets
- ❖ 1 cut in wedges lemon

Cooking Instructions:

1. In a shallow dish, combine all the seasonings; then press the salmon filets, flesh side down, into the seasonings to coat well.

2. Set to sear on medium heat and add the oil. Place the salmon, skin side up, in the pot and cook until blackened for about 3 minutes.

3. Turn the filets over and cook for another 5 to 7 minutes or until they reach desired doneness.

4. Serve immediately with lemon wedges.

Shrimp Etouffee

Preparation time: 30 minutes

Cooking time: 30 minutes

Overall time: 60 minutes

Serves: 2 to 4 people

Recipe Ingredients:
- ¼ cup of olive oil
- ¼ cup of flour
- 1 chopped stalk celery
- 1 chopped green bell pepper
- 2 chopped jalapeno peppers
- ½ chopped onion
- 4 chopped garlic cloves
- 2 cups of clam juice
- 1 tablespoon of cajun seasoning
- ½ teaspoon of celery seed
- 1 tablespoon of paprika
- 2 pounds of shell on shrimp (deveined)
- 3 chopped green onions
- Hot sauce to taste

Cooking Instructions:

1. Add the oil to the cooking pot and set to sauté on medium heat, then whisk in the flour until it is smooth. Cook until it is deep brown, whisking frequently for about 10 minutes.

2. Add celery, bell pepper, jalapeno, and onion and cook 4 minutes, stirring occasionally. Add the garlic and cook for more 2 minutes.

3. Slowly stir in clam juice, a little at a time, until combined. The sauce should look like syrup, add more juice if needed.

4. Add Cajun seasoning, celery seed, and paprika and mix well. Add the shrimp. Cover, reduce heat to low and cook for 10 minutes. Stir in green onions and hot sauce then serve over rice immediately.

Pepper Smothered Cod

Preparation time: 10 minutes

Cooking time: 20 minutes

Overall time: 30 minutes

Serves: 2 to 4 people

Recipe Ingredients:

- ¼ cup of olive oil
- ½ cup of chopped red onion
- 2 teaspoons of chopped garlic
- ½ cup of chopped red bell pepper
- ½ cup of chopped green bell pepper
- Salt and pepper (to taste)
- 4 tablespoons of flour
- 2 cups of low sodium chicken broth
- ½ cup tomato, seeded & chopped
- 2 teaspoons of fresh thyme, chopped
- 4 cod filets

Cooking Instructions:

1. Set to sauté on med-high heat and add oil to the cooking pot. After that, add the onion and garlic and cook while stirring for 1 minute.

2. Add the peppers, salt, and pepper and cook, stirring frequently for about 2 to 3 minutes, or until peppers start to get tender.

3. Stir in the flour and cook until it turns a light brown. Pour in the broth and cook, stirring until it's smooth and the sauce starts to thicken.

4. Then stir in tomato and thyme. Season the fish with salt and pepper and place in the pot; add the lid.

5. Cook for about 3 to 4 minutes, then turn the fish over and cook for another 3 to 4 minute or until fish flakes is easy with a fork. Transfer the fish to serving plates and top with sauce. Serve immediately.

Easy Clam Chowder

Preparation time: 10 minutes

Cooking time: 3 hrs.

Overall time: 3 hrs. 10 minutes

Serves: 2 to 4 people

Recipe Ingredients:
- ❖ 5 chopped slices bacon
- ❖ 2 finely chopped cloves garlic,
- ❖ ½ chopped onion
- ❖ ½ teaspoon of thyme
- ❖ 1 cup of low sodium chicken broth
- ❖ 4 ounces cream cheese
- ❖ 18 ounces of chopped and drained clams
- ❖ 1 bay leaf
- ❖ 3 cups of cauliflower (separated in florets)
- ❖ 1 cup of unsweetened almond milk
- ❖ 1 cup of heavy cream
- ❖ 2 tablespoons of chopped fresh parsley

Cooking Instructions:
1. Add the bacon to the cooking pot and set to sauté on med-high heat. Cook until it becomes crisp, then transfer to a paper-towel lined plate.

2. Pour out all but 3 tablespoons of the fat. Add the onion and garlic and cook for 2 to 3 minutes until onion is transparent.

3. Add the thyme and cook for 1 minute more. Add the broth, cream cheese, clams, bay leaf, and cauliflower, and then mix until it's combined.

4. Add the lid and set to slow cook on low. Cook for about 2 to 3 hours until cauliflower is tender. Stir in the milk and cream and cook until it is heated through.

5. Scoop into bowls and top with bacon and parsley and serve warm.

CHAPTER 3 - POULTRY RECIPES
Sour Cream and Cheese Chicken

Preparation time: 6 minutes

Cooking time: 25 minutes

Overall time: 31 minutes

Serves: 2 to 4 people

Recipe Ingredients:
- ❖ Nonstick cooking spray
- ❖ 1 cup of sour cream
- ❖ 2 teaspoons of garlic powder
- ❖ 1 teaspoon of seasoned salt
- ❖ ½ teaspoon of pepper
- ❖ 1 ½ cups of parmesan cheese (divided)
- ❖ 3 pounds of boneless chicken breasts

Cooking Instructions:
1. Spray the cooking pot with cooking spray.

2. In a medium bowl, combine sour cream, garlic powder, seasoned salt, pepper, and 1 cup of parmesan cheese and mix very well.

3. Place the chicken in the cooking pot and spread the sour cream mixture over the top and sprinkle with remaining parmesan cheese.

4. Add the tender-crisp lid and set to bake on 375°F. Bake chicken 25 to 30 minutes until it is cooked through.

5. Set cooker to broil and cook another 2 to 3 minutes until top is lightly browned.

6. Serve immediately.

Turkey Breakfast Sausage

Preparation time: 6 minutes

Cooking time: 10 minutes

Overall time: 16 minutes

Serves: 4 to 8 people

Recipe Ingredients:
- ❖ Nonstick cooking spray
- ❖ 1 pound of ground turkey
- ❖ ½ teaspoon of sage
- ❖ ½ teaspoon of marjoram
- ❖ ¾ teaspoon of thyme
- ❖ ¼ teaspoon of cayenne pepper
- ❖ ¼ teaspoon of allspice
- ❖ ¼ teaspoon of black pepper
- ❖ ¾ teaspoon of salt
- ❖ 1 finely chopped clove garlic
- ❖ ¼ cup of maple syrup

Cooking Instructions:

1. Start by spraying the fryer basket with cooking spray and place in the cooking pot.

2. In a large bowl, mix all ingredients until it is combined, then form into 8 patties.

3. Place the sausage patties in the fryer basket in a single layer. Add the tender-crisp lid and set to air-fry on 375°F.

4. Cook for about 10 minutes or until it is browned on the outside and cooked through, turning over halfway through cooking time.

5. Serve immediately.

Spicy Southern Chicken

Preparation time: 6 minutes

Cooking time: 20 minutes

Overall time: 26 minutes

Serves: 2 to 4 people

Recipe Ingredients:
- ❖ 1 teaspoon of thyme
- ❖ Nonstick cooking spray
- ❖ 1 teaspoon of onion powder
- ❖ 1 teaspoon of garlic powder
- ❖ 1 teaspoon of oregano
- ❖ 2 teaspoons of paprika
- ❖ 1 teaspoon of salt
- ❖ 1 teaspoon of pepper + ½ teaspoon cayenne pepper
- ❖ 2 pounds of boneless & skinless chicken breasts

Cooking Instructions:

1. Start by spraying the cooking pot with cooking spray.

2. In a medium bowl, combine the spices and seasonings until well mixed. Coat all sides of the chicken with the spice mixture and place in the pot.

3. Add the tender-crisp lid and set to roast on 425°F. Cook 20 minutes or until chicken is cooked through and let rest 5 minutes before serving.

4. Serve immediately and enjoy

Beacon and Cranberry Stuffed Turkey Breast

Preparation time: 30 minutes

Cooking time: 1 hr.

Overall time: 1 hr. 30 minutes

Serves: 2 to 4 people

Recipe Ingredients:

- ❖ ¼ ounces of dried porcini mushrooms
- ❖ 1 slice bacon, thick cut, chopped
- ❖ ¼ cup of finely chopped shallot
- ❖ 2 tablespoons of chopped dried cranberries
- ❖ 1 teaspoon of finely chopped fresh sage
- ❖ ½ cup of bread crumbs
- ❖ 1 tablespoon of chopped fresh parsley
- ❖ 3 tablespoons of low sodium chicken broth
- ❖ 2 pounds of boneless turkey breast
- ❖ 2 tablespoons of butter, soft
- ❖ ½ teaspoon of salt

Cooking Instructions:

1. In a small bowl, add the mushrooms and enough hot water to cover them. Let it sit for 15 minutes, then drain and chop them.

2. Set the cooker to sauté on medium heat; add the bacon and cook until crisp and then transfer to a paper-towel lined plate.

3. Add the shallots and cook until they start to brown, about 3 to 5 minutes. Add the cranberries, sage, and mushrooms and cook, stirring frequently, 2 to 3 minutes.

4. Stir in bread crumbs, parsley, bacon, and broth and mix well. Transfer to a bowl to cool.

5. Remove the skin from the turkey, in one piece, do not discard. Butterfly the turkey breast and place between 2 sheets of plastic wrap. Pound out to ¼-inch thick.

6. Spread the stuffing over the turkey, leaving a ¾-inch border. Start with a short end and roll up the turkey, then wrap the skin back around the roll.

7. Use butcher string to tie the turkey, place in the cooking pot and rub with butter and sprinkle with salt, then add the tender-crisp lid and set to roast on 400°F.

8. Cook for 20 minutes, then decrease the heat to 325°F and cook for another 10 to 15 minutes or until juices run clear. Let rest 10 minutes before slicing and serving.

Red Chili Chicken

Preparation time: 10 minutes

Cooking time: 1 hr.

Overall time: 1 hr. 10 minutes

Serves: 3 to 6 people

Recipe Ingredients:

- ❖ 1 tablespoon of olive oil
- ❖ 1 ¼ cups of mexican red chili sauce
- ❖ 2 tablespoons of cider vinegar
- ❖ ½ teaspoon of cloves
- ❖ ½ teaspoon of allspice
- ❖ 1 teaspoon of cinnamon
- ❖ ¼ teaspoon of cumin
- ❖ ¼ teaspoon of pepper
- ❖ ¼ teaspoon of oregano
- ❖ 1 teaspoon of garlic, chopped fine
- ❖ 3 pounds of chicken thighs
- ❖ 1 teaspoon of salt

Cooking Instructions:

1. Add oil to the cooking pot and set to sauté on medium heat.

2. Add the chili sauce, vinegar, cloves, allspice, cinnamon, cumin, pepper, oregano, and garlic. Bring to a simmer and cook for 5 minutes. Turn off heat and let cool.

3. Sprinkle chicken with salt and place in a large Ziploc bag, add the sauce and turn to coat. Refrigerate at least 1 hour or overnight is best.

4. Place the chicken, skin side up, in the cooking pot. Add the tender-crisp lid and set to roast on 350°F.

5. Then cook for about 34 to 50 minutes or until cooked through and juices run clear. Serve garnished with cilantro and enjoy.

Tangy Chicken and Rice

Preparation time: 5 minutes

Cooking time: 1 hr.

Overall time: 1 hr. 5 minutes

Serves: 3 to 6 people

Recipe Ingredients:

- ❖ 3 teaspoons of chili powder
- ❖ 1 teaspoon of paprika
- ❖ 1 teaspoon of garlic powder
- ❖ 1 teaspoon of onion powder
- ❖ ¼ teaspoon of cayenne pepper
- ❖ 1 teaspoon of salt
- ❖ ¼ teaspoon of pepper
- ❖ 6 boneless & skinless chicken thighs
- ❖ 2 tablespoon of olive oil
- ❖ 1 cup of rice uncooked
- ❖ 2 ¼ cups of chicken broth, low sodium
- ❖ 1 tablespoon + 2 teaspoons of fresh lime juice
- ❖ 2 tablespoons of chopped cilantro

Cooking Instructions:

1. In a small bowl, combine the spices and seasonings, mix well. Use half the mixture to season the chicken on both sides.

2. Add the oil to the pot and set to sauté on medium heat. Cook chicken until it is browned for about 3 to 4 minutes per side, then transfer to a plate.

3. Add rice, the remaining seasoning mixture, broth, and 1 tablespoon lime juice to the pot, mix well. Place the chicken on top of the rice.

4. Add the lid and cook 20 to 25 minutes until chicken is cooked through and the liquid is absorbed.

5. Transfer chicken to serving plates. Fluff the rice with a fork, top with cilantro and remaining lime juice. Serve immediately.

Turkey Rellenos

Preparation time: 10 minutes

Cooking time: 20 minutes.

Overall time: 30 minutes

Serves: 2 to 4 people

Recipe Ingredients:

- ❖ Nonstick cooking spray
- ❖ 4 poblano chilies
- ❖ ½ pound of hot Italian turkey sausage (casings removed)
- ❖ 1 cup of cottage cheese, reduced fat, drained
- ❖ ½ cup of grated mozzarella cheese

Cooking Instructions

1. Lightly spray fryer basket with cooking spray and place in the cooking pot.

2. Split the chilies with a knife and remove the seeds, do not remove the stems. Place in the basket.

3. Add the tender-crisp lid and set to broil, then cook chilies until skin chars on all sides.

4. Transfer to a large Ziploc bag and seal. When the chilies have cooled, carefully remove the skin.

5. Remove the fryer basket and set to cooker to sauté on med-high heat. Cook sausage until it is no longer pink, now transfer to a medium bowl.

6. Add the cottage cheese to the sausage and mix very well.

7. Spoon the sausage mixture into the chilies and lay them in the basket, spit side up. Sprinkle the mozzarella cheese over.

8. Add the basket back to the pot and set to bake on 350°F. Bake for 15 minutes until the cheese is melted and bubbly. Serve immediately.

Cheesy Chicken and Mushrooms

Preparation time: 5 minutes

Cooking time: 30 minutes.

Overall time: 35 minutes

Serves: 2 to 4 people

Recipe Ingredients:
- ❖ Nonstick cooking spray
- ❖ 1 ½ cups of sliced mushrooms,
- ❖ ¼ cup of chopped ham
- ❖ 4 boneless & skinless chicken breasts
- ❖ ½ teaspoon of garlic powder
- ❖ ¼ teaspoon of pepper
- ❖ 1 can cream of chicken soup (reduced fat)
- ❖ ¾ cup of skim milk
- ❖ ½ teaspoon of thyme
- ❖ ½ teaspoon of onion powder
- ❖ ¼ cup of grated mozzarella cheese

Cooking Instructions:
1. Start by spraying the cooking pot with cooking spray.

2. Set to sauté on med-high heat and add the mushrooms and ham and cook for about 5 to 7 minutes while stirring occasionally until mushrooms start to brown.

3. After that, transfer to a bowl. Season both sides of the chicken with garlic powder and pepper and place in the pot.

4. Serve the mushroom mixture over the top. Then in a medium bowl, beat together soup, milk, thyme, and onion powder. Pour over mushrooms and top with cheese.

5. Add the tender-crisp lid and set to bake on 350°F. Cook for about 25 to 30 minutes or until chicken is cooked through. Serve immediately.

Cheesy Chipotle Chicken

Preparation time: 10 minutes

Cooking time: 35 minutes.

Overall time: 45 minutes

Serves: 3 to 6 people

Recipe Ingredients:

- ❖ 15 ounces of fire roasted tomatoes
- ❖ ¼ cup of chopped red onion
- ❖ 1 garlic clove
- ❖ ½ cup of packed chopped cilantro,
- ❖ 2 chipotle chili peppers in adobo sauce
- ❖ 1 teaspoon of adobo sauce
- ❖ 1 teaspoon of fresh lime juice
- ❖ 1 teaspoon of salt
- ❖ 1 ½ pounds of chicken (cut in 3-inch pieces)
- ❖ 1 cup of grated monterey Jack cheese

Cooking Instructions

1. Start by adding the tomatoes, onion, garlic, cilantro, chipotle peppers, lime juice, and salt to a food processor or blender.

2. Pulse until vegetables are chopped but not until the salsa is smooth.

3. Place the chicken in the cooking pot. Pour the salsa over the tops. Turn the chicken to coat with salsa on all sides.

4. Add the tender-crisp lid and set to bake on 350°F. Bake 25 minutes and remove the lid and sprinkle the cheese over the top.

5. Recover and bake for another 10 minutes or until chicken is cooked through and cheese is melted and starting to brown. Serve immediately.

Chicken Cutlets in Dijon Sauce

Preparation time: 10 minutes

Cooking time: 1 hr. 15 minutes

Overall time: 1 hr. 25 minutes

Serves: 3 to 6 people

Recipe Ingredients:
- ❖ 2 boneless and skinless chicken breasts,
- ❖ 2 tablespoons of olive oil (divided)
- ❖ ½ teaspoon of salt
- ❖ ¼ teaspoon of pepper
- ❖ ½ tablespoon of lemon zest
- ❖ 1 finely chopped garlic clove
- ❖ 1 tablespoon of chopped fresh rosemary
- ❖ 1 tablespoon of chopped fresh parsley
- ❖ 2 tablespoons of flour
- ❖ Nonstick cooking spray
- ❖ 1 sliced thin shallot
- ❖ ½ lemon juiced
- ❖ ½ cup of dry white wine
- ❖ 1 teaspoon of Dijon mustard

Cooking Instructions:
1. Place chicken between 2 pieces of plastic wrap and pound to ½-inch thick, then place them in a large bowl.

2. Top the chicken with oil, salt, pepper, zest, garlic, rosemary, and parsley; cover and refrigerate for 1 hour or overnight.

3. Place the flour in a shallow dish and dredge both sides of chicken. Let it sit for about 2 to 3 minutes.

4. Lightly spray the fryer basket with cooking spray. Then place the chicken in the basket and add the tender-crisp lid and set to air-fry on 350°F.

5. Cook chicken for about 3 to 5 minutes per side until it is golden brown and cooked through. Transfer to plate and keep warm.

6. Set cooker to sauté on medium heat. Add the oil and shallot and cook until shallot softens. Stir in lemon juice, wine, and mustard and cook until it is reduced slightly for about 2 to 3 minutes.

7. After that, transfer chicken to serving plates and top with sauce. Serve immediately.

Cran-Apple Turkey Cutlets

Preparation time: 11 minutes

Cooking time: 10 minutes

Overall time: 21 minutes

Serves: 2 to 4 people

Recipe Ingredients:

- ❖ Nonstick cooking spray
- ❖ 4 turkey breast cutlets
- ❖ 1 finely chopped granny smith apple,
- ❖ 2 tablespoons of dried cranberries
- ❖ 2 teaspoons of fine grated orange peel
- ❖ 2 tablespoon of orange juice

Cooking Instructions:

1. Start by spraying the cooking pot with cooking spray and set to sauté on medium heat.

2. Add the turkey cutlets and cook for about 3 to 4 minutes per side or until it is no longer pink, then transfer to serving plate and keep warm.

3. Add remaining ingredients to the pot and stir to mix. Cook while stirring occasionally for about 4 minutes or until apples are tender.

4. Spoon over turkey and serve immediately.

Spanish Chicken and Olives

Preparation time: 1 hr.

Cooking time: 50 minutes

Overall time: 1 hr. 50 minutes

Serves: 2 to 4 people

Recipe Ingredients:

- ¼ cup of extra virgin olive oil
- ¼ cup of red wine vinegar
- 2 teaspoons of chopped fresh oregano
- 1 teaspoon of salt
- ½ teaspoon of garlic powder
- 1/8 teaspoon of pepper
- 3 bay leaves
- ½ cup of golden raisins
- ¼ cup of green olives, pitted & halved
- 3 pounds of chicken
- ½ cup of dry white wine
- 2 tablespoons of brown sugar

Cooking Instructions:

1. In a medium bowl, whisk together oil, vinegar, oregano, salt, garlic powder, pepper, bay leaves, raisins, and olives.

2. Prick the chicken with a fork all over and add to marinade, turning to coat. Cover and refrigerate for 1 hour or overnight.

3. Transfer the chicken to the cooking pot. Whisk the wine and brown sugar into the marinade and pour over the top.

4. Add the tender-crisp lid and set to bake on 350°F. Bake for about 45 to 50 minutes, basting occasionally or until chicken is cooked through.

5. Remove bay leaves before serving. Serve and enjoy.

Lemon, Barley and Turkey Soup

Preparation time: 11 minutes

Cooking time: 4 hours

Overall time: 4 hrs. 11 minute

Serves: 3 to 6 people

Recipe Ingredients:

- ❖ 3 tablespoons of extra virgin olive oil
- ❖ 1 finely chopped onion
- ❖ 3 finely chopped garlic cloves
- ❖ 1 teaspoon of turmeric
- ❖ ½ teaspoon of cumin
- ❖ ½ teaspoon of ginger
- ❖ ½ teaspoon of salt
- ❖ ½ teaspoon of pepper
- ❖ 6 cups of low sodium chicken broth
- ❖ 6 to 8 strips of lemon peel, (pith removed)
- ❖ 1 cup of barley
- ❖ 2 cups of cooked & chopped turkey
- ❖ 2 tablespoons of lemon juice
- ❖ ¼ cup of chopped fresh parsley
- ❖ ¼ cup of chopped cilantro

Cooking Instructions:

1. Add the oil to the cooking pot and set to saute on med-heat.

2. Add the onion and cook for about 2 to 3 minutes until it becomes translucent. Then stir in the garlic and cook for 1 minute more.

3. Add turmeric, cumin, ginger, and salt, stir to combine. Pour in the broth, zest, and barley.

4. Add the lid and set to slow cook on low. Then cook for about 3 to 3 ½ hours or until barley is tender.

5. When the barley is cooked, add the turkey, lemon juice, parsley, cilantro, salt, and pepper and cook for 30 minutes or until heated through. Remove the lemon peel before serving.

Easy Chicken Goulash

Preparation time: 11 minutes

Cooking time: 25 minutes

Overall time: 36 minutes

Serves: 2 to 4 people

Recipe Ingredients:

- ❖ 1 tablespoon of paprika
- ❖ ¼ teaspoon of salt
- ❖ ¼ teaspoon of pepper
- ❖ 1 ½ pounds boneless and skinless chicken breasts (cut in ½-inch pieces)
- ❖ 1 tablespoon of olive oil
- ❖ ½ cup of chopped onion
- ❖ 2 cups of sliced mushrooms
- ❖ 14 ½ ounces of diced tomatoes
- ❖ 1 teaspoon of garlic powder
- ❖ 1 can of low sodium condensed cream of mushroom soup
- ❖ ½ cup of water

Cooking Instructions:

1. In a medium bowl, combine paprika, salt and pepper, mix well. Add chicken and toss to coat.

2. Add the oil to the cooking pot and set to sauté on medium heat. Add the chicken and the onion and cook for 5 minutes, stirring frequently.

3. Stir in mushrooms and cook another 3 to 4 minutes until chicken is browned.

4. Add remaining ingredients and stir to mix. Cover, reduce heat to low and cook for about 15 to 20 minutes or until chicken is cooked through. Serve immediately.

Hula Chicken

Preparation time: 6 minutes

Cooking time: 10 minutes

Overall time: 16 minutes

Serves: 2 to 4 people

Recipe Ingredients:

- ❖ 2 tablespoons of low sodium soy sauce
- ❖ 1 tablespoon of brown sugar
- ❖ 1 teaspoon of fine grated fresh ginger
- ❖ 3 finely chopped cloves garlic
- ❖ ¼ teaspoon of pepper
- ❖ 4 boneless and skinless chicken breasts
- ❖ Nonstick cooking spray
- ❖ 1 sliced green onion

Cooking Instructions:

1. Add the soy sauce, brown sugar, ginger, garlic, and pepper to a large Ziploc bag, seal and turn to mix.

2. Add the chicken, reseal and refrigerate at least 4 hours or overnight. Spray the cooking rack with cooking spray and place in the cooking pot.

3. Place the chicken on the rack and add the tender-crisp lid. Set to roast on 325°F.

4. Cook 5 to 6 minutes per side until chicken is no longer pink, transfer to plates and garnish with green onions.

5. Serve immediately.

Shredded Chicken and Black Beans

Preparation time: 5 minutes

Cooking time: 4 hrs.

Overall time: 4 hrs. 5 minutes

Serves: 2 to 4 people

Recipe Ingredients:

- ❖ 16 ounces of fresh salsa
- ❖ 15 ounces of rinsed and drained black beans,
- ❖ 1 pound of boneless & skinless chicken thighs
- ❖ 1/3 cup of grated cheddar cheese, (reduced fat)
- ❖ 1 teaspoon of cumin
- ❖ ½ teaspoon of chili powder
- ❖ 1/8 teaspoon of salt
- ❖ 1/8 teaspoon of pepper

Cooking Instructions

1. Place the salsa, beans, and chicken in the cooking pot.

2. Then add the lid and set to slow cook on high and cook for 3 ½ hours or until chicken is tender.

3. Transfer chicken to a cutting board and use 2 forks to shred, return to the pot.

4. Stir in remaining ingredients and mix well. Cook for another 15 minutes or until cheese is melted.

5. Serve immediately.

West African Chicken and Sweet Potato Stew

Preparation time: 11 minutes

Cooking time: 25 minutes

Overall time: 36 minutes

Serves: 2 to 4 people

Recipe Ingredients:
- 3 tablespoon of olive oil
- 2 pounds of chicken legs & thighs
- ½ teaspoon of salt
- 1 sliced onion
- 3-inch piece of ginger (peeled and chopped fine)
- 6 finely chopped garlic cloves
- 2 pounds of peeled & cubed sweet potatoes
- 1 quart of low sodium chicken broth,
- 15 ounces of crushed tomatoes
- 1 cup of peanut butter
- 1 cup of peanuts, roasted
- 1 tablespoon of coriander
- 1 teaspoon of cayenne pepper
- ½ teaspoon of pepper
- ¼ cup of chopped cilantro

Cooking Instructions:

1. Start by adding the oil to the cooking pot and set to sauté on med-high. Season the chicken with salt and add them to the pot, don't over crowd them. Then cook for about 2 to 3 minutes per sides or until its browned.

2. Transfer to a plate, add the onion and cook, while stirring frequently for about 3 to 4 minutes, scraping up any brown bits from the bottom of the pot.

3. Add the ginger and garlic and cook another 2 minutes. Add the sweet potatoes, broth, tomatoes, peanut butter, peanuts, coriander, cayenne, and pepper, stir well.

4. Include the chicken back to the pot, add the lid and set to pressure cook on high. Then set the timer for 30 minutes. When the timer goes off, use manual release to remove the lid.

5. If the chicken is not tender, cook for another 10 minutes. Transfer the chicken to a bowl and let cool enough to handle.

6. Slice the meat off the bones and put it back in the pot. Adjust seasonings if needed, stir in the cilantro and serve immediately.

Apricot BBQ Duck Legs

Preparation time: 5 minutes

Cooking time: 8 hrs.

Overall time: 8 hrs. 5 minutes

Serves: 3 to 6 people

Recipe Ingredients:
- ❖ Nonstick cooking spray
- ❖ 2 cups of spicy BBQ sauce
- ❖ 1 cup of apricot preserves
- ❖ 1 teaspoon of ginger
- ❖ 1 tablespoon of garlic powder
- ❖ 2 tablespoons of worcestershire sauce
- ❖ 4 pounds of duck legs

Cooking Instructions:

1. Start by spraying the cooking pot with cooking spray.

2. In a medium bowl, whisk together BBQ sauce, preserves, ginger, garlic powder, and Worcestershire until it is thoroughly combined. Reserve ½ cup of the sauce.

3. Add the duck to the cooking pot and pour the sauce over and stir to coat the duck.

4. Add the lid and select slow cook on low. Then cook for about 6 to 8 hours or until duck is tender.

5. Add the tender-crisp lid and set to broil. Cook for another 2 to 3 minutes to caramelize the duck legs. Turn the legs over and repeat process.

6. Serve immediately and enjoy.

Pizza Stuffed Chicken

Preparation time: 10 minutes

Cooking time: 20 minutes

Overall time: 30 minutes

Serves: 2 to 4 people

Recipe Ingredients:

- ❖ 2 tablespoons of parmesan cheese (divided)
- ❖ Nonstick cooking spray
- ❖ 2 boneless & skinless chicken breasts
- ❖ ½ teaspoon of oregano
- ❖ 12 slices of turkey pepperoni
- ❖ ½ cup of grated mozzarella cheese (divided)
- ❖ 3 tablespoons of whole-wheat bread crumbs
- ❖ 4 b of low sodium marinara sauce

Cooking Instructions:

1. Place the rack in the cooking pot. Spray the fryer basket with cooking spray.

2. Cut each breast in half horizontally. Place between 2 sheets of plastic wrap and pound out to ¼-inch thick.

3. Sprinkle 1 tablespoon of parmesan and the oregano over chicken; top each cutlet with 3 slices of pepperoni and 1 tablespoon mozzarella and roll up.

4. In a shallow dish, combine bread crumbs and remaining parmesan, mix well.

5. Coat chicken rolls in bread crumbs and place, seam side down, in the fryer basket. Lightly spray with cooking spray.

6. Add the tender-crisp lid and set to air fry on 400°F and cook 15 minutes.

7. Open the lid and top each chicken roll with 1 tablespoon marinara sauce and remaining mozzarella. Cook for 5 to 7 minutes until chicken is cooked through and cheese is melted.

8. Serve immediately.

Sesame Crusted Chicken

Preparation time: 5 minutes

Cooking time: 10 minutes

Overall time: 15 minutes

Serves: 3 to 6 people

Recipe Ingredients:

- ❖ 1 teaspoon of garlic powder
- ❖ 2 tablespoons of sesame seeds
- ❖ 1 teaspoon of thyme
- ❖ Nonstick cooking spray
- ❖ 1 egg
- ❖ 2 tablespoons of water
- ❖ ¼ teaspoon of salt
- ❖ ¼ teaspoon of pepper
- ❖ ½ cup of Italian-seasoned bread crumbs
- ❖ 4 boneless & skinless chicken breasts

Cooking Instructions:

1. Spray the fryer basket with cooking spray and place it in the cooking pot.

2. In a shallow dish, whisk egg and water until it is thoroughly combined. In another shallow dish, combine remaining ingredients, mix well.

3. Place chicken between 2 sheets of plastic wrap and pound out to ¼-inch thick.

4. Dip chicken first in the egg then coat with bread crumb mixture and place in the fryer basket.

5. Add the tender-crisp lid and set to air fry on 375°F. Cook chicken for 10 minutes, turning over halfway through cooking time, or until chicken is no longer pink.

6. Serve. Immediately and enjoy.

Ginger Orange Chicken Tenders

Preparation time: 5 minutes

Cooking time: 25 minutes

Overall time: 30 minutes

Serves: 2 to 4 people

Recipe Ingredients:

- ❖ Nonstick cooking spray
- ❖ 1 ½ pounds of chicken tenders
- ❖ 1 cup of orange juice
- ❖ 2 teaspoons of low sodium tamari
- ❖ ½ teaspoon of ginger
- ❖ 11 ounces of drained mandarin oranges

Cooking Instructions:

1. Start by spraying the fryer basket with cooking spray.

2. Place chicken in a single layer in the basket, these may need to be cooked in batches.

3. Add the tender-crisp lid and set to air-fry on 350°F and cook for 10 minutes, turning over halfway through cooking time.

4. Add all the tenders to the cooking pot. Then in a small bowl, whisk together orange juice, soy sauce, and ginger.

5. Pour over chicken and stir to coat all the pieces. Set to sauté on medium heat.

6. Cover and cook chicken while stirring occasionally for about 10 minutes. After 10 minutes, add the orange slices and cook for another 5 minutes.

7. Serve immediately and enjoy.

Turkey and Cabbage Enchiladas

Preparation time: 11 minutes

Cooking time: 30 minutes

Overall time: 41 minutes

Serves: 2 to 4 people

Recipe Ingredients:
- ❖ Nonstick cooking spray
- ❖ 8 large cabbage leaves
- ❖ 1 tablespoon of olive oil
- ❖ ½ cup of chopped onion
- ❖ ½ red chopped bell pepper
- ❖ 3 finely chopped cloves garlic
- ❖ 2 teaspoons of cumin
- ❖ 1 tablespoon of chili powder
- ❖ 1 teaspoon of salt
- ❖ ¼ teaspoon of crushed red pepper flakes
- ❖ 2 cups of cooked & shredded turkey
- ❖ 1 cup of enchilada sauce, sugar free
- ❖ ½ cup of cheddar cheese, fat free, grated

Cooking Instructions

1. Start by spraying a small baking dish with cooking spray. Bring a large pot of water to boil. Add cabbage leaves and cook for 30 seconds.

2. After that, transfer leaves to paper towel lined surface and pat dry. Add the oil to the cooking pot and set to sauté on medium heat.

3. Add the onion, bell pepper, and garlic and cook while stirring occasionally, until onions are transparent for about 5 minutes.

4. Stir in cumin, chili powder, salt, red pepper flakes, and turkey. Cook just until it heat through then transfer mixture to a bowl. Add the rack to the cooking pot.

5. Lay cabbage leaves on work surface and divide turkey mixture evenly between leaves. Fold in the sides and roll up. Place in the prepared dish, seam side down and pour the enchilada sauce over the top and sprinkle with cheese.

6. Place dish on the rack and add the tender-crisp lid. Set to bake on 400°F and cook enchiladas for about 15 to 20 minutes or until cheese is melted and bubbly.

7. Let it rest for 5 minutes before serving. Serve immediately and enjoy your meal.

Caprese Stuffed Chicken

Preparation time: 6 minutes

Cooking time: 15 minutes

Overall time: 21 minutes

Serves: 2 to 4 people

Cooking Ingredients:
- ❖ Nonstick cooking spray
- ❖ 4 boneless & skinless chicken breasts
- ❖ 2 Roma tomatoes, sliced ¼-inch thick
- ❖ ¾ cup of grated mozzarella cheese
- ❖ 1 teaspoon of salt
- ❖ ½ teaspoon of pepper
- ❖ ¼ cup of chopped fresh basil
- ❖ 2 tablespoons of dark balsamic vinegar

Cooking Instructions:
1. Start by spraying the cooking pot with cooking spray.

2. Cut the chicken horizontally to create a pocket, being careful not to cut all the way through.

3. Stuff the pockets with tomatoes and cheese, secure with a toothpick. Season the chicken with salt and pepper.

4. Set cooker to sauté on medium heat and add the chicken and sear on one side until light brown, for about 5 minutes. Carefully turn the chicken over.

5. Add the tender-crisp lid and to bake on 400°F, then cook chicken for about 10 minutes or until it is cooked through.

6. Transfer to serving plates and top with basil and a drizzle of the balsamic vinegar.

7. Serve immediately.

Spanish Chicken and Rice

Preparation time: 6 minutes

Cooking time: 25 minutes

Overall time: 31 minutes

Serves: 2 to 4 people

Recipe Ingredients:

- ❖ 1 tablespoon of olive oil
- ❖ 4 boneless & skinless chicken breasts
- ❖ 1 finely chopped onion
- ❖ 1 finely chopped bell pepper,
- ❖ 1 cup of instant brown rice
- ❖ ¾ cup of low sodium chicken broth
- ❖ 14 ½ ounces of diced and undrained tomatoes,
- ❖ 1 teaspoon of thyme
- ❖ ¼ teaspoon of crushed red pepper flakes
- ❖ ¼ teaspoon of salt
- ❖ ½ teaspoon of pepper

Cooking Instructions:

1. Add the oil to the cooking pot and set to sauté on medium heat. Add chicken and cook until it is browned on both sides for about 5 minutes per side.

2. After that, transfer to a plate. Add onion and bell pepper and cook for about 5 to 6 minutes or until tender.

3. Place the chicken back in the pot and add rice, broth, tomatoes, and seasonings, stir to combine.

4. Reduce heat to low, cover, and cook for 10 minutes or until chicken is cooked through.

5. Turn off the cooker and let sit, covered, 5 minutes. Fluff rice with a fork and serve immediately.

Italian Chicken Muffins

Preparation time: 11 minutes

Cooking time: 25 minutes

Overall time: 36 minutes

Serves: 2 to 4 people

Recipe Ingredients:
- ❖ Nonstick cooking spray
- ❖ 4 chicken breast halves, boneless & skinless
- ❖ ½ teaspoon of salt, divided
- ❖ ½ teaspoon of pepper, divided
- ❖ 1/3 cup of part-skim ricotta cheese
- ❖ ¼ cup of mozzarella cheese, grated
- ❖ 2 tablespoons of parmesan cheese
- ❖ ½ teaspoon of Italian seasoning
- ❖ ½ teaspoon of garlic powder
- ❖ 2 tablespoons of whole-wheat panko bread crumbs
- ❖ 1 tablespoon of light butter, melted
- ❖ Paprika for sprinkling

Cooking Instructions:

1. Place the rack in the cooking pot and spray 4 cups of a 6- cup muffin tin.

2. Lay chicken between 2 sheets of plastic wrap and pound to ¼-inch thick then season with ¼ teaspoon of salt and pepper.

3. In a medium bowl, combine ricotta, mozzarella, parmesan, Italian seasoning, garlic powder, and remaining salt and pepper, mix well.

4. Spoon evenly onto centers of chicken and wrap chicken around filling and place, seam side down, in prepared muffin cups.

5. In a small bowl, stir together bread crumbs and butter, sprinkle over the chicken then top with paprika.

6. Place muffin tin on rack and add the tender-crisp lid. Set to bake on 350°F and cook chicken for about 25 to 30 minutes or until chicken is cooked through. Serve immediately.

CHAPTER 4 - BEEF LAMB AND PORK RECIPES
Ham, Bean and Butternut Soup

Preparation time: 21 minutes

Cooking time: 4 hrs. 30 minutes

Overall time: 4 hrs. 51 minutes

Serves: 3 to 6 people

Recipe Ingredients:
- ❖ 2 tablespoons of extra virgin olive oil
- ❖ 2 cups of chopped onion
- ❖ 3 bay leaves
- ❖ 2 chopped stalks celery
- ❖ 4 finely chopped garlic cloves,
- ❖ 3 ½ cups of sugar pumpkin, cut in 1-inch pieces
- ❖ ½ pound of ham hock
- ❖ 8 cups of chicken broth, low sodium
- ❖ 1 chopped tomato
- ❖ ½ teaspoon of thyme
- ❖ 30 ounces of drained & rinsed cannellini beans,
- ❖ ¼ teaspoon of pepper
- ❖ 4 Swiss chard leaves, rib removed & chopped

Cooking Instructions:
1. Add the oil to the cooking pot and set to sauté on med-high heat.

2. Add the onion and bay leaves and cook, stirring frequently, until onion starts to soften for about 2 to 3 minutes. Add celery and cook for 3 minutes, then add garlic and cook 1 minute more.

3. Add pumpkin, broth, tomatoes, thyme, and ham hock, stir to mix. Add the lid and set to slow cook on high; cook for 4 hours or until ham if falling off the bone.

4. Transfer ham hock to a plate to cool slightly. Stir the beans, pepper, and chard into the soup. Recover and let it cook until chard is wilted.

5. Remove the ham from the bone and chop it. Return it to the pot and continue cooking until heated through. Remove bay leaves before serving.

Simple Beef and Shallot Curry

Preparation time: 1 hr.

Cooking time: 40 minutes

Overall time: 1 hr. 40 minutes

Serves: 2 to 4 people

Recipe Ingredients:
- ❖ 1 pound of beef stew meat
- ❖ ¼ teaspoon of salt
- ❖ 1/8 teaspoon of turmeric
- ❖ 2 tablespoons of olive oil
- ❖ 2 tablespoons of sliced shallots,
- ❖ 1 tablespoon of fresh grated ginger
- ❖ 1 tablespoon of finely chopped garlic
- ❖ 3 cups of water
- ❖ 2 teaspoons of fish sauce
- ❖ 8 peeled & left whole shallots
- ❖ ½ teaspoon of chili powder

Cooking Instructions:
1. In a large bowl, combine beef, salt, and turmeric, use your fingers to massage the seasonings into the meat, then cover and refrigerate for 1 hour.

2. Add the oil to the cooking pot and set to sauté on med-high. Add the sliced shallot and cook until golden brown, for about 6 to 8 minutes, then transfer to a bowl.

3. Add the garlic and ginger to the pot and cook 1 minute or until fragrant.

4. Add the beef and cook until no pink shows, for about 5 to 6 minutes. Stir in the water and fish sauce until combined.

5. Add the lid and set to pressure cook on high. Set the timer for 20 minutes. When the timer goes off, use manual release to remove the pressure.

6. Set back to sauté on med-high and add the fried shallots, whole shallots, and chili powder.

7. Cook, stirring frequently, until shallots are soft and sauce has thickened, for about 10 minutes. Serve immediately.

Polynesian Pork Burger

Preparation time: 5 minutes

Cooking time: 10 minutes

Overall time: 15 minutes

Serves: 3 to 6 people

Recipe Ingredients:

- ❖ 1 pound of ground pork
- ❖ ¼ cup green onion, chopped fine
- ❖ 1/8 tablespoon of all spice
- ❖ 1/8 tablespoon of salt
- ❖ 1/8 tablespoon of pepper
- ❖ ½ tablespoon of ginger
- ❖ 4 pineapple rings
- ❖ ¼ cup of barbecue sauce
- ❖ 4 burger buns
- ❖ 4 large lettuce leaves
- ❖ ¼ pound of sliced thin ham

Cooking Instructions:

1. Start by spraying the rack with cooking spray and place it in the cooking pot.

2. In a large bowl, combine pork, green onion, allspice, salt, pepper, and ginger until thoroughly mixed and form into 4 patties.

3. Place the patties on the rack and brush the tops with barbecue sauce. Add the tender-crisp lid and set to broil.

4. Cook patties for about 5 to 7 minutes, then flip and brush with barbecue sauce, cook for another 5 to 7 minutes.

5. Place the patties on the bottom of the cooking pot. Spray the rack with cooking spray again.

6. Lay the pineapple rings on the rack. Cook 3 to 5 minutes per side. Transfer pineapple and patties to a serving plate and let sit 5 minutes.

7. Place the buns on the rack, cut side up, and toast. To serve; top bottom bun with lettuce, then patty, barbecue sauce, ham, pineapple and top bun. Then Serve immediately.

Ham, Ricotta and Zucchini Fritters

Preparation time: 11 minutes

Cooking time: 10 minutes

Overall time: 21 minutes

Serves: 2 to 4 people

Recipe Ingredients:

- ❖ 1 ½ tablespoons of unsalted butter
- ❖ 1/3 cup of milk
- ❖ ½ cup of ricotta cheese
- ❖ 2 eggs
- ❖ 1 ½ teaspoons of baking powder
- ❖ ½ teaspoons of salt
- ❖ ¼ teaspoon of pepper
- ❖ 1 cup of flour
- ❖ ¼ cup of fresh chopped basil
- ❖ 3 ounces of ham (cut in strips)
- ❖ ½ zucchini (cut into matchsticks)

Cooking Instructions:

1. Spray the fryer basket with cooking spray and place in the cooking pot.

2. Place the butter in a large microwave safe bowl and microwave until melted.

3. Whisk milk and ricotta into melted butter until it is smooth. Then whip in eggs until it is thoroughly combined.

4. Stir in baking powder, salt, and pepper until combined. Stir in flour, until it is combined.

5. Fold in basil, ham and zucchini until distributed evenly. Drop batter by ¼ cups into fryer basket, these will need to be cooked in batches.

6. Add the tender-crisp lid and set to air fry on 375°F. Cook fritters for about 4 to 5 minutes per side until golden brown and cooked through. Serve immediately.

Healthier Meatloaf

Preparation time: 10 minutes

Cooking time: 6 hrs.

Overall time: 6 hrs. 10 minutes

Serves: 3 to 6 people

Recipe Ingredients:

- ❖ Nonstick cooking spray
- ❖ 1 pound of lean ground pork
- ❖ 1 cup of oats
- ❖ 8 ounces of tomato sauce (divided)
- ❖ 1 finely chopped onion
- ❖ ½ cup of grated zucchini (excess liquid squeezed out)
- ❖ 1 chopped finely garlic clove
- ❖ 1 lightly beaten egg
- ❖ 1 teaspoon of salt
- ❖ 1/8 teaspoon of pepper
- ❖ ½ teaspoon of Italian seasoning

Cooking Instructions:

1. Start by spraying the cooking pot with cooking spray.

2. In a large bowl, combine pork, oats, half the tomato sauce, onion, zucchini, garlic, egg, salt, pepper, and Italian seasoning, mix very well.

3. Fold a large sheet of foil in half, then in half again. Place along the bottom up two sides of the cooking pot.

4. Add the pork mixture and form into a loaf shape. Spoon remaining tomato sauce over the top.

5. Add the lid and set to slow cook on low and cook for 6 hours or until meatloaf is cooked through.

6. Use the foil sling to remove the meatloaf from the cooking pot. Let it rest for 5 minutes before slicing and serving. Serve and enjoy immediately.

Basque Lamb Stew

Preparation time: 20 minutes

Cooking time: 6 hrs.

Overall time: 6 hrs. 20 minutes

Serves: 3 to 6 people

Recipe Ingredients:
- ❖ 3 ½ pounds of lamb shoulder (cut in 2-inch pieces)
- ❖ 6 cloves garlic, chopped fine (divided)
- ❖ 1 tablespoon of chopped fresh rosemary
- ❖ ½ cup of dry white wine
- ❖ 2 tablespoons of olive oil
- ❖ 1 chopped onion
- ❖ ½ teaspoon of salt
- ❖ 2 teaspoons of sweet paprika
- ❖ 10 ounces of roasted red bell peppers (cut in ½-inch strips)
- ❖ 1 tomato peeled, seeded, and chopped
- ❖ 2 tablespoons of chopped fresh parsley,
- ❖ 1 bay leaf
- ❖ 1 cup of dry red wine, full bodied
- ❖ 1 cup of low sodium chicken broth
- ❖ ½ teaspoon of pepper

Cooking Instructions:
1. Place the lamb in a large bowl and add half the garlic, the rosemary, wine. Cover and refrigerated for about 2 to 3 hours.

2. Add the oil to the cooking pot and set to sear and add the lamb, season with salt, and cook just until brown on the outside, transfer to bowl.

3. Add the onion to the pot and cook, stirring to scrape up the brown bits on the bottom of the pot. Cook until onions are soft. Then add the garlic and cook 1 minute more.

4. Return the lamb to the pot along with remaining ingredients, stir to mix well.

5. Add the lid and set to slow cook on high. Cook for about 4 to 6 hours until lamb is tender. Stir to mix, discard the bay leaf and serve.

Sausage and Roasted Red Pepper Linguine

Preparation time: 15 minutes

Cooking time: 15 minutes

Overall time: 30 minutes

Serves: 2 to 4 people

Recipe Ingredients:

- ❖ 1 tablespoon of extra virgin olive oil
- ❖ ¾ pound of Italian sausage
- ❖ 3 finely chopped garlic cloves
- ❖ 1 cup of chopped roasted red bell peppers
- ❖ 1 tablespoon of capers
- ❖ ½ cup of pitted & halved black olives
- ❖ 3 seeded & chopped tomatoes
- ❖ ¼ cup of fresh chopped basil
- ❖ 1 pound of cooked & drained linguine

Cooking Instructions:

1. Start by adding the oil to the cooking pot and set to sauté on medium heat.

2. Add sausage and break it up while it's cooking. When it starts to brown; add the garlic and cook for 1 minute more.

3. Stir in the peppers, capers, and olives and cook stirring for 2 minutes. After 2 minutes, increase heat to high and add tomatoes and basil, cook for 2 minutes more.

4. Add the pasta to the sausage mixture and toss to combine. Serve immediately.

Beef, Barley and Mushroom Stew

Preparation time: 16 minutes

Cooking time: 1 hr. 15 minutes

Overall time: 1 hr. 31 minutes

Serves: 4 to 8 people

Recipe Ingredients:

- ❖ ½ teaspoon of pepper
- ❖ ½ cup of sour cream
- ❖ 8 small sprigs fresh dill
- ❖ 1 teaspoon of salt
- ❖ 3 cups of chopped onions
- ❖ 1 pound of sliced mushrooms
- ❖ 1 quart of low sodium beef broth
- ❖ 2 tablespoons of unsalted butter
- ❖ 2 pounds of cubed beef chuck
- ❖ 3 cups of water
- ❖ 2 teaspoons of marjoram
- ❖ 1 cup of pearl barley
- ❖ 1 cup of chopped carrot
- ❖ 3 cups of peeled & chopped turnips

Cooking Instructions:

1. Start by adding butter to the cooking pot and set to sauté on medium heat.

2. Working in batches, cook the beef until brown on all sides, seasoning with salt as it cooks, then transfer browned beef to a bowl.

3. Add the onions and cook, stirring up brown bits from the bottom of the pot, for about 5 to 6 minutes or until they begin to brown.

4. Add the mushrooms and increase heat to med-high. Cook for about 2 to 3 minutes.

5. Add the beef back to the pot and stir in marjoram, broth, and water, stir to mix.

6. Add the lid and set to pressure cook on high. Set timer for 30 minutes. When timer goes off use quick release to remove the pressure.

7. Stir in barley, turnips, and carrots. Add the lid and pressure cook on high another 30 minutes.

8. When the timer goes off, use quick release to remove the pressure. Scoop into bowls and garnish sour cream and dill.

9. Serve immediately and enjoy.

Pepper Crusted Tri Tip Roast

Preparation time: 1 hr.

Cooking time: 45 minutes

Overall time: 1 hr. 45 minutes

Serves: 4 to 8 people

Recipe Ingredients:
- ❖ 1 tablespoon of pepper
- ❖ 1 teaspoon of cayenne pepper
- ❖ 3 pounds of tri-tip roast
- ❖ 1 tablespoon of salt
- ❖ Nonstick cooking spray
- ❖ 1 tablespoon of oregano
- ❖ 1 teaspoon of rosemary
- ❖ ½ teaspoon of sage
- ❖ 1 tablespoon of garlic powder
- ❖ 1 tablespoon of onion powder

Cooking Instructions:
1. Combine all the spices in a small bowl until it is thoroughly mixed up together.

2. Place the roast on baking sheet and massage the rub mix into all sides; cover and let it sit for 1 hour.

3. Lightly spray the cooking pot with cooking spray, then set to sear.

4. Add the roast and brown all sides. Add the tender-crisp lid and set to roast on 300°F.

5. Cook for about 20 to 40 minutes or until meat thermometer reaches desired temperature for doneness.

6. Temperature should read at least (120°F); for a rare roast (130°F); for medium-rare and (140°F for medium,

7. Remove roast from cooking pot, tent with foil and let rest for about 10 to 15 minutes. Slice across the grain and serve immediately.

Beef Brisket and Carrots

Preparation time: 35 minutes

Cooking time: 8 hrs. 15 minutes

Overall time: 8 hrs. 50 minutes

Serves: 5 to 10 people

Recipe Ingredients:

- ❖ 4 to 5 of beef brisket
- ❖ 1 ½ teaspoons of salt
- ❖ 3 sliced onions
- ❖ 6 finely chopped garlic cloves
- ❖ 1 sprig thyme
- ❖ 1 sprig rosemary
- ❖ 4 bay leaves
- ❖ 2 cups of low sodium beef broth
- ❖ 3 carrots (peeled & sliced ½-inch thick)
- ❖ 1 tablespoon of mustard

Cooking Instructions:

1. Use a sharp knife and score the fat side of the brisket in parallel lines, being careful to only slice through the fat, not the meat.

2. Repeat to create a cross-hatch pattern. Sprinkle with salt and let sit for 30 minutes.

3. After 30 minutes, set the cooker to sear on med-high and lay brisket, fat side down in the pot.

4. Cook 5 to 8 minutes to render the fat. Turn the brisket over and brown the other side. Transfer to a plate.

5. Add the onions and season with salt. Cook for about 5 to 8 minutes while stirring frequently, until onions are browned. Then add the garlic and cook for 1 minute more.

6. Stir in remaining ingredients; add the brisket back to the pot, pushing it down to cover as much as possible by the broth.

7. Add the lid and set to slow cook on low. Cook for about 8 to 9 hours or until brisket is tender.

8. Transfer brisket to cutting board and tent with foil. Let it rest for about 10 to 15 minutes.

9. Slice across the grain to serve with carrots, onions and some of the cooking liquid.

10. Serve and enjoy your meal immediately.

African Pork Stew

Preparation time: 11 minutes

Cooking time: 8 hrs.

Overall time: 8 hrs. 11 minutes

Serves: 6 people

Recipe Ingredients:

- ❖ 2 bay leaves
- ❖ 1 chopped onion
- ❖ 2 tablespoons of finely chopped garlic
- ❖ 1 teaspoon of adobo powder
- ❖ 2 pounds of cubed pork loin
- ❖ 2 tablespoons of olive oil
- ❖ 3 slices of chopped bacon
- ❖ 2 peeled & cubed potatoes
- ❖ 1 pounds of sliced smoked sausage
- ❖ 1 can of diced tomatoes
- ❖ 14½ ounces of yellow hominy, drained
- ❖ 3 cups of red beans, drained & rinsed

Cooking Instructions:

1. Start by adding all the ingredients to the cooking pot and stir to combine.

2. Add the lid and set to slow cook on low. Then cook for about 6 to 8 hours or until meat and vegetables are tender.

3. Remove the bay leaves and stir thoroughly well. Once done, serve and enjoy.

Cuban Marinated Pork

Preparation time: 10 minutes

Cooking time: 10 hrs.

Overall time: 10 hrs. 10 minutes

Serves: 4 to 8 people

Recipe Ingredients:
- ❖ 4 pounds of bone in pork shoulder
- ❖ 1½ teaspoons of salt
- ❖ 1 teaspoon of pepper
- ❖ ½ cup of fresh lime juice
- ❖ ¾ cup of fresh orange juice
- ❖ 1 orange zest
- ❖ 1 lime zest of
- ❖ ½ cup of olive oil
- ❖ 8 finely chopped garlic cloves
- ❖ 2 teaspoons of oregano
- ❖ 2 teaspoons of cumin
- ❖ ¼ cup of cilantro, chopped

Cooking Instructions
1. Use a sharp knife to score the pork.

2. Add remaining ingredients to the cooking pot and stir to mix very well, then top with pork.

3. Add the lid and set to slow cook on low and cook for about 8 to 10 hours or until meat is almost tender.

4. Line a baking sheet with foil and place the pork on it and drain cooking liquid into a large bowl.

5. Add the pork back to the pot and add the tender-crisp lid and set to roast on 400°F. Cook pork for about 15 to 20 minutes or until it is browned.

6. Transfer pork to a cutting board and let it rest for 10 minutes. Slice and serve topped with some of the reserved cooking liquid. Serve and enjoy.

Beef Bourguignon

Preparation time: 21 minutes

Cooking time: 9 hrs.

Overall time: 9 hrs. 21 minutes

Serves: 3 to 6 people

Recipe Ingredients:

- ❖ 5 finely chopped slices bacon,
- ❖ 3 pounds of beef chuck (cut in 1-inch cubes)
- ❖ 1 cup of red cooking wine
- ❖ 2 cups of low sodium beef broth
- ❖ ½ cup of tomato sauce
- ❖ ¼ cup of soy sauce
- ❖ ¼ cup of flour
- ❖ 3 finely chopped garlic cloves
- ❖ 2 tablespoons of finely chopped thyme
- ❖ 5 sliced carrots
- ❖ 1 pounds of baby potatoes
- ❖ 8 ounces of sliced mushrooms
- ❖ 2 tablespoons of freshly chopped parsley,

Cooking Instructions:

1. Add the bacon to the cooking pot and set to sauté on med high and cook until it becomes crisp, then transfer to a bowl.

2. Season the beef with salt and pepper; add to the pot and brown on all sides again, add to the bacon.

3. Add the wine to the pot and stir to scrape up the brown bits from the bottom of the pot and cook for about 2 to 3 minutes to reduce. Stir in broth, tomato sauce, and soy sauce and slowly whisk in flour.

4. Add the beef and bacon back to the pot along with remaining ingredients, except parsley, and stir to mix very well.

5. Add the lid and set to slow cook on low and cook for about 8 to 10 hours or until beef is tender. Stir and serve garnished with parsley. Yummy!

Tex Mex Beef Stew

Preparation time: 16 minutes

Cooking time: 25 minutes

Overall time: 41 minutes

Serves: 4 to 10 people

Recipe Ingredients:
- ❖ 2 teaspoons of cumin
- ❖ 1 teaspoon of salt
- ❖ 1 teaspoon of garlic powder
- ❖ 2 tablespoons of coconut oil
- ❖ 1 pound of lean ground beef
- ❖ 1 pound of boneless beef chuck (cut in 1-inch cubes)
- ❖ 2 cups of chopped sweet onions,
- ❖ 1 seeded & chopped yellow bell pepper
- ❖ 1 seeded & chopped orange bell pepper
- ❖ 1 peeled & chopped sweet potato
- ❖ 2 (28) ounces cans crushed of tomatoes
- ❖ 1 cup of low sodium beef broth
- ❖ 3 chopped chipotle peppers in adobo sauce
- ❖ ¼ cup of chopped cilantro (divided)

Cooking Instructions:
1. In a small bowl, combine cumin, salt, and garlic powder. Add oil to the cooking pot and set to sauté on med-high heat.

2. Add the ground beef and half the spice mixture and cook until beef is no longer pink. Use a slotted spoon to transfer beef to a bowl.

3. Add beef chuck and remaining spice mixture and cook until meat is browned on all sides.

4. Add the ground beef back to the pot; then add remaining ingredients, except cilantro, and mix to combine

5. Add the lid and set to pressure cook on high. Set timer for 12 minutes. When the timer goes off, use manual release to remove the pressure.

6. Stir in 2 tablespoons cilantro. Ladle into bowls and garnish with remaining cilantro. Serve immediately.

Polish Sausage and Sauerkraut

Preparation time: 11 minutes

Cooking time: 7 hrs.

Overall time: 7 hrs. 11 minutes

Serves: 3 to 6 people

Recipe Ingredients:

- ❖ 2 tablespoons of olive oil
- ❖ 1 onion chopped
- ❖ 2 bay leaves
- ❖ 1 cup of dry red wine
- ❖ ½ pound of chopped bacon
- ❖ 1 cup of low sodium beef broth
- ❖ 1 chopped head cabbage
- ❖ 1 pound of rinsed & drained sauerkraut
- ❖ ½ pound of smoked Polish sausage (cut in 1-inch pieces)

Cooking Instructions:

1. Add the oil to the cooking pot and set to sauté on medium heat.

2. Add the onions and cook, stirring occasionally, until onions are golden. Use a slotted spoon to transfer onions to a bowl.

3. Add bacon to the pot and cook for about 2 to 3 minutes. Add sausage and cook for about 5 minutes until it is nicely browned.

4. Use a slotted spoon to transfer meat to the bowl with onions; then drain off any remaining fat.

5. Add the cabbage, sauerkraut, and broth to the pot and mix well. Add the lid and set to slow cook on low and cook for 4 hours.

6. Stir in the onion mixture, bay leaves, and wine. Recover and cook for another 2 to 3 hours or until vegetables are tender. Remove bay leaves, stir and serve immediately.

Beef in Basil Sauce

Preparation time: 6 minutes

Cooking time: 15 minutes

Overall time: 21 minutes

Serves: 2 to 4 people

Recipe Ingredients:
- ❖ 2 tablespoons of olive oil
- ❖ 2 sliced thin shallots
- ❖ 7 sliced garlic cloves
- ❖ 1 tablespoon of peeled & grated fresh ginger
- ❖ ½ sliced thin red bell pepper
- ❖ 1 pounds of lean ground beef
- ❖ 2 teaspoons of brown sugar
- ❖ 2 tablespoons of fish sauce
- ❖ 6 tablespoons of low sodium soy sauce
- ❖ 3 teaspoons of oyster sauce
- ❖ 2 tablespoons of asian garlic chili paste
- ❖ ½ cup of low sodium beef broth
- ❖ ¼ cup of water
- ❖ 1 teaspoon of cornstarch
- ❖ 1 cup of chopped basil leaves
- ❖ Cooked Jasmine rice (for serving)

Cooking Instructions:

1. Start by adding the oil to the cooking pot and set to sauté on med-high heat. Add the shallots, garlic, ginger, and bell peppers to the pot and cook while stirring frequently for 3 minutes.

2. Use a slotted spoon to transfer mixture to a bowl. Then increase heat to high and add the ground beef, cook, breaking it up with a spoon until beef is no longer pink.

3. In a small bowl, whisk together brown sugar, fish sauce, soy sauce, oyster sauce, cornstarch, broth, and water until smooth.

4. Add the pepper mixture back to the pot and pour the sauce over and cook while stirring for 2 minutes or until sauce has thickened. Stir in basil and cook until wilted for about 2 minutes. Serve over hot rice and enjoy.

Moroccan Beef

Preparation time: 10 minutes

Cooking time: 7 hrs. 40 minutes

Overall time: 7 hrs. 50 minutes

Serves: 10 people

Recipe Ingredients:
- ❖ 2 sliced tomatoes
- ❖ 2 tablespoons of honey
- ❖ 1 tablespoon of harissa paste
- ❖ ¼ cup of chopped dates
- ❖ 2 cups of cooked rice
- ❖ ¼ cup of chopped cilantro
- ❖ ¼ cup of toasted sesame seeds,
- ❖ 1 tablespoon of ras el hanout
- ❖ ½ teaspoon of cinnamon
- ❖ ½ pound of sliced dried apricots
- ❖ 1 seeded & sliced yellow bell pepper
- ❖ 1 cup of sliced thin onion
- ❖ 2 pounds of cubed beef chuck roast
- ❖ 1 tablespoon of salt
- ❖ 1 tablespoon of unsalted butter
- ❖ 3 chopped garlic cloves

Cooking Instructions:
1. Start by seasoning the meat with salt and mix thoroughly well to combine. After that, add the butter to the cooking pot and set to sauté on med-high heat.

2. Once butter has melted, add meat and cook, stirring occasionally until it becomes browned on all sides.

3. Then in a large bowl, combine tomatoes, honey, harissa, ras el hanout seasoning, and cinnamon, mix well.

4. Stir in apricots, bell pepper, onion, garlic, and dates and pour over the beef. Add the lid and set to slow cook on low.

5. Cook for about 7 to 9 hours until beef and vegetables are tender. After that, divide rice evenly among serving plates.

6. Top with beef mixture and garnish with cilantro and sesame seeds. Serve immediately.

Beer Braised Bacon and Cabbage

Preparation time: 6 minutes

Cooking time: 15 minutes

Overall time: 21 minutes

Serves: 2 to 4 people

Recipe Ingredients:

- ❖ 1 tablespoon of butter
- ❖ 1 sliced in strips onion
- ❖ 3 ½ ounces of chopped bacon
- ❖ 1 sliced in strips savoy cabbage
- ❖ 1 cup of blonde beer

Cooking Instructions:

1. Add the butter to the cooking pot and set to sauté on medium heat.

2. Once butter has melted, add onion and bacon and cook while stirring occasionally or until onions is soft for about 5 minutes.

3. Add the cabbage and beer, stir to mix. Add the lid and set to pressure cook on high and set the timer for 3 minutes.

4. When the timer goes off, use manual release to remove the pressure. Stir and serve immediately.

Tender Beef and Onion Rings

Preparation time: 16 minutes

Cooking time: 25 minutes

Overall time: 41 minutes

Serves: 4 to 6 people

Recipe Ingredients:
- ❖ 2 pounds cubed chuck roast
- ❖ ¼ cup of low sodium soy sauce
- ❖ 1 tablespoon of lemon juice
- ❖ ½ teaspoon of pepper
- ❖ 1 cup of water
- ❖ 3 tablespoons of olive oil
- ❖ 3 fine chopped garlic cloves
- ❖ 1 sliced & separated onion in rings

Cooking Instructions:

1. In a large bowl, combine beef, soy sauce, lemon juice, and pepper, mix well, then cover and let it sit for 1 hour.

2. Add the beef mixture to the cooking pot. Stir in water. Add the lid and set to pressure cook on high.

3. Set timer for 20 minutes. When the timer goes off, use natural release to remove the pressure.

4. Use a slotted spoon to transfer beef to a bowl. Set cooker to sauté on medium heat.

5. Cook until sauce reduces and thickens for about 3 to 4 minutes. Stir in oil and garlic.

6. Add the beef back to the pot and cook until sauce turns a light brown, about 4 to 5 minutes.

7. Add the onion rings and cook for 2 minutes, or until onions are almost soft. Serve immediately.

Balsamic Braised Lamb Shanks

Preparation time: 11 minutes

Cooking time: 1 hr.

Overall time: 1 hr. 11 minutes

Serves: 4 people

Recipe Ingredients:

- ❖ 1 tablespoon of coconut oil
- ❖ 3 peeled & chopped carrots
- ❖ 3 chopped stalks celery
- ❖ 4 fine chopped garlic cloves
- ❖ 1 chopped onion
- ❖ 1 tablespoon of balsamic vinegar
- ❖ 2 tablespoons of chopped fresh Italian parsley,
- ❖ 3 pounds of lamb shanks
- ❖ 1 teaspoon of salt (divided)
- ❖ ½ teaspoon of pepper (divided)
- ❖ 1 tablespoon of tomato paste
- ❖ 14 ounces of fire roasted tomatoes
- ❖ 1 cup of low sodium beef broth
- ❖ ½ teaspoon of crushed red pepper flakes

Cooking Instructions:

1. Season lamb with salt and pepper. Add oil to the cooking pot and set to sauté on med-high.

2. Add the lamb and brown on all sides and transfer to a large serving plate.

3. Add the carrots, celery, garlic, and onion and season with salt and pepper. Cook, while stirring frequently or until onion is transparent.

4. Add tomato paste, and roasted tomatoes, stir to mix. Return the lamb to the pot along with broth, pepper flakes, and vinegar.

5. Add the lid and set to pressure cook on high. Set the timer for 45 minutes. When the timer goes off, use natural release to remove the pressure.

6. Transfer lamb to a serving plate and spoon sauce over them Garnish with parsley and serve immediately.

Spiced Lamb Shoulder

Preparation time: 6 minutes

Cooking time: 1 hr.

Overall time: 1 hr. 6 minutes

Serves: 4 to 8 people

Recipe Ingredients:

- ❖ 1 tablespoon of olive oil
- ❖ 3 ½ pounds of lamb shoulder, bone-in, rolled & tied
- ❖ 1 cinnamon stick
- ❖ 2 dried, broken in pieces red chilies
- ❖ 1 tablespoon of fresh ginger, grated
- ❖ 1 tablespoons of garlic paste
- ❖ ½ cup of water
- ❖ 1 teaspoon of cumin
- ❖ 2 teaspoons of coriander
- ❖ 1 teaspoon of salt
- ❖ 3 lightly crushed peppercorns

Cooking Instructions:

1. Start by adding the oil to the cooking pot and set to sauté on med-high. Add the lamb and sear on all sides. Again, add the tender-crisp lid and set to roast on 350°F.

2. Roast the lamb for 20 minutes and then transfer the lamb to a plate. After that, set the cooker back to sauté on medium heat.

3. Add the cinnamon stick and red chilies to the pot and cook for about 1 to 2 minutes until aromatic.

4. Stir in ginger, garlic paste, and water and bring to a boil. Whisk in the cumin, coriander, salt, and peppercorns and let the sauce cook for 5 to 10 minutes. Add the lamb back to the sauce and add the lid and set to pressure cook on high.

5. Set the timer for 20 minutes. When the timer goes off, use manual release to remove the pressure. Transfer the lamb to a cutting board, tent with foil and let it rest 10 minutes.

6. Discard the cinnamon stick and pour the sauce in a blender, process until smooth. To serve, slice the meat and top with the sauce. Enjoy.

Smoky Sausage and Potato Soup

Preparation time: 16 minutes

Cooking time: 4 hrs.

Overall time: 4 hrs. 16 minutes

Serves: 4 people

Recipe Ingredients:

- ❖ 2 peeled & chopped carrots

- ❖ 2 stalks celery, chopped

- ❖ 2 russet potatoes (cut in 1-inch cubes)

- ❖ 2 cup of chopped baby spinach

- ❖ 2 cup of low sodium chicken broth

- ❖ 1 cup of skim milk

- ❖ 1 pound of smoked sausage (cut in bite-sized pieces)

- ❖ 1 ½ cups of chopped fine onion,

Cooking Instructions:

1. Add the sausage, onion, carrot, celery, potatoes and broth to the cooking pot.

2. Add the lid and set to slow cook on high and cook for 4 hours or until sausage and vegetables are tender.

3. About 10 minutes before the end of cooking time, add ½ cup cooking liquid to a small bowl and whisk in the milk.

4. Add the milk mixture to the pot along with the spinach and cook until spinach wilts. Serve immediately.

CHAPTER 5- VEGAN AND VEGETABLE RECIPES
Eggplant and Penne Pot

Preparation time: 10 minutes

Cooking time: 20 minutes

Overall time: 30 minutes

Serves: 4 people

Recipe Ingredients:
- ❖ 1 finely chopped clove garlic
- ❖ 1 eggplant (cut in ¼-inch pieces)
- ❖ 2 teaspoons of sugar
- ❖ 1 ½ cups baby spinach
- ❖ 1 chopped red bell pepper,
- ❖ ½ teaspoon of salt
- ❖ ½ teaspoon of pepper
- ❖ 2 tablespoons of olive oil
- ❖ 1 chopped onion
- ❖ 10 ounces of tomato sauce
- ❖ 20 ounces of cooked and drained penne pasta

Cooking Instructions:
1. Add oil to the cooking pot and set to sauté on med-high.

2. Add onions and cook for about 2 to 3 minutes or until they start to soften then add garlic and cook for 1 minute more.

3. Add the eggplant, peppers, salt, and pepper and cook for about 5 minutes while stirring occasionally.

4. Mix in the tomato sauce and sugar and cook for about 3 to 4 minutes or until eggplant is tender.

5. Stir in the spinach and cook for about 2 to 3 minutes until it wilts and is tender. Stir in pasta and cook just until heated through. Serve immediately.

Mushroom Leek Soup with Parmesan Croutons

Preparation time: 11 minutes

Cooking time: 15 minutes

Overall time: 26 minutes

Serves: 4 to 8 people

Recipe Ingredients:

- ❖ 4 slices brioche bread (cut in ¼-inch cubes)
- ❖ 2 tablespoons of olive oil
- ❖ 2 tablespoons of parmesan cheese
- ❖ 2 teaspoons of pepper
- ❖ 3 tablespoons of butter
- ❖ 4 trimmed leeks, (sliced into ½-inch thick)
- ❖ 4 cups of sliced cremini mushrooms
- ❖ ½ cup of white wine
- ❖ 3 tablespoons of flour
- ❖ 4 cups of low sodium chicken broth
- ❖ 2/3 cup of milk
- ❖ ½ teaspoon of salt

Cooking Instructions:

1. In a large bowl, mix bread, olive oil, parmesan, and pepper, toss to coat bread.

2. Set cooker to sauté on medium heat. Add the bread and cook for about 5 minutes while stirring frequently or until its toasted, then transfer to a plate.

3. Add the butter to the cooking pot and let it melt. Add the leeks and cook for 5 minutes or until translucent. Add the mushrooms and cook for another 5 minutes.

4. Stir in wine scraping up any browned bits on the bottom of the pan and cook just until liquid is almost evaporated then stir in flour for 1 minute.

5. Add the broth, stirring until no lumps remain. Add the milk and salt and let it cook for 5 minutes.

6. Use an immersion blender, or transfer to a blender, and process until it becomes almost smooth. Then scoop into bowls and top with croutons. Serve immediately.

Cheesy Corn Casserole

Preparation time: 6 minutes

Cooking time: 4 hrs.

Overall time: 4 hrs. 6 minutes

Serves: 4 to 8 people

Recipe Ingredients:

- ❖ 1 ¾ pounds of corn
- ❖ ¼ cup of sliced butter
- ❖ ¼ cup of heavy cream
- ❖ 8 ounces of cubed cream cheese
- ❖ 1 cup of grated cheddar cheese
- ❖ ½ teaspoon of salt
- ❖ Nonstick cooking spray
- ❖ ¼ teaspoon of pepper

Cooking Instructions:

1. Spray the cooking pot with cooking spray. Then add all the ingredients to the cooking pot and whisk to mix.

2. Add the lid and set to slow cook on low. Cook for about 3 ½ to 4 hours, stirring occasionally or until all the cheese has melted and casserole is hot.

3. Stir well before serving. Serve immediately and enjoy.

Pumpkin Soup

Preparation time: 11 minutes

Cooking time: 8 hrs.

Overall time: 8 hrs. 11 minutes

Recipe Ingredients:

- ❖ 15 ounces of pumpkin
- ❖ 1 cup of chopped celery
- ❖ ½ cup of chopped fine carrots
- ❖ ½ cup of chopped fine onion
- ❖ ¼ teaspoon of salt
- ❖ ½ teaspoon of oregano
- ❖ ½ teaspoon of rosemary
- ❖ ¼ teaspoon of red pepper
- ❖ ¼ teaspoon of ginger
- ❖ 28 ounces of vegetable broth
- ❖ ¼ cup of whipped cream
- ❖ 3 tablespoons of toasted pumpkin seeds

Cooking Instructions:

1. Add all ingredients, except whipped cream and pumpkin seeds, to the cooking pot and mix well.

2. Add the lid and set to slow cook on low. Cook for about 6 to 8 hours. After that, stir in whipped cream until thoroughly combined.

3. Ladle into bowls and top with pumpkin seeds.

4. Serve immediately.

Southwest Tofu Steaks

Preparation time: 11 minutes

Cooking time: 30 minutes

Overall time: 41 minutes

Serves: 4 people

Recipe Ingredients:

- ❖ Nonstick cooking spray
- ❖ 1 pkg. of drained & pressed firm tofu
- ❖ 1 tablespoon of chili powder
- ❖ 1 teaspoon of cumin
- ❖ ½ teaspoon of garlic powder
- ❖ 1 teaspoon of paprika
- ❖ ½ tablespoon of oregano
- ❖ ½ tablespoon of ground coriander
- ❖ ½ teaspoon of salt
- ❖ 3 tablespoons of extra virgin olive oil
- ❖ 2 tablespoons of water

Cooking Instructions:

1. Line a baking sheet with foil. Spray fryer basket with cooking spray. Slice tofu in half horizontally. Then slice each half horizontally again.

2. In a small bowl combine remaining ingredients and mix very well. Spread mixture over both sides of tofu and place on prepared pan and let it sit 30 to 45 minutes.

3. Place tofu in fryer basket and add the tender-crisp lid. Set to air-fry on 400°F.

4. Cook tofu 30 minutes, turning over halfway through cooking time. Season with salt and pepper and serve immediately.

Stir Fried Veggies

Preparation time: 11 minutes

Cooking time: 5 minutes

Overall time: 16 minutes

Serves: 6 people

Recipe Ingredients:

- ❖ 1 tablespoon of olive oil
- ❖ 2 bell peppers, (cut in strips)
- ❖ 1 cup of sugar snap peas
- ❖ 1 cup of sliced thin carrots
- ❖ 1 cup of mushrooms, sliced thin
- ❖ 2 cups of broccoli (separate into small florets)
- ❖ 1 cup of baby corn
- ❖ ½ cup of water chestnuts
- ❖ ¼ cup of soy sauce
- ❖ 3 finely chopped garlic cloves
- ❖ 3 tablespoons of brown sugar
- ❖ 1 teaspoon of sesame oil
- ❖ ½ cup of vegetable broth
- ❖ 1 tablespoon of cornstarch
- ❖ ¼ cup of sliced green onions

Cooking Instructions:

1. Add oil to the cooking pot and set to saute on med-high heat.

2. Add bell pepper, peas, carrots, mushrooms, broccoli, corn, and water chestnuts.

3. Cook and stir frequently for about 2 to 3 minutes or until almost tender.

4. Then in a small bowl, whisk together soy sauce, garlic, brown sugar, sesame oil, broth, and cornstarch until it is combined.

5. Pour over vegetables and cook, stirring, until sauce has thickened. Then spoon onto serving plates and garnish with green onions. Serve and enjoy.

Hot and Sour Soup

Preparation time: 10 minutes

Cooking time: 20 minutes

Overall time: 30 minutes

Serves: 5 people

Recipe Ingredients:

- ❖ 3 ½ cups of low sodium chicken broth (divided)
- ❖ ½ pound of firm tofu (cut in 1-inch cubes)
- ❖ ¼ pound of sliced mushrooms
- ❖ 3 tablespoons of low sodium soy sauce
- ❖ 3 tablespoons of vinegar
- ❖ 1 teaspoon of ginger
- ❖ ½ teaspoon of pepper
- ❖ 2 tablespoons of cornstarch
- ❖ 1 lightly beaten egg,
- ❖ ½ cup of fresh bean sprouts
- ❖ ½ teaspoon of sesame oil

Cooking Instructions:

1. Add 3 ¼ cups of broth, tofu, mushrooms, soy sauce, vinegar, ginger, and pepper to the cooking pot and stir thoroughly well.

2. Set to sauté on medium heat and bring to a boil. After that, whisk together remaining broth and cornstarch in a small bowl until its smooth.

3. Reduce heat to low and whisk in cornstarch mixture until thickened. Slowly stir in egg to form egg "ribbons".

4. Add bean sprouts and cook for 1 to 2 minutes or until heated through while stirring occasionally then stir in sesame oil. Serve immediately.

Cheesy Spicy Pasta

Preparation time: 11 minutes

Cooking time: 40 minutes

Overall time: 51 minutes

Serves: 6 people

Recipe Ingredients:

- ❖ 1 ½ cups of low-fat cottage cheese
- ❖ ½ cup of ricotta cheese
- ❖ ½ cup of greek yogurt
- ❖ 2 cups of grated mozzarella cheese (divided)
- ❖ ¼ cup of chopped fresh parsley
- ❖ 2 cups of baby spinach
- ❖ 1 tablespoon of butter
- ❖ 1 chopped onion
- ❖ 2 tablespoons of garlic, chopped fine
- ❖ 14 ½ ounces of fire-roasted tomatoes
- ❖ 8 ounces of tomato sauce
- ❖ ½ teaspoons of red pepper flakes
- ❖ 1 ½ teaspoons of oregano
- ❖ 1 teaspoon of rosemary
- ❖ ½ teaspoon of salt
- ❖ ½ teaspoon of pepper
- ❖ ¾ pound of cooked & drained whole grain pasta
- ❖ 6 tablespoons of parmesan cheese

Cooking Instructions:

1. In a medium bowl, combine cottage cheese, ricotta, yogurt, 1 cup of mozzarella, parsley, and spinach and mix thoroughly well.

2. Add the butter to the cooking pot and set to sauté on med-high. Once the butter melts, add the onion and cook until it becomes translucent.

3. Add the garlic and cook for 1 minute more. After that, stir in tomatoes, tomato sauce, and seasonings, reduce heat to low and simmer 5 minutes.

4. Stir in the pasta and the ricotta mixture, mix well. Top with remaining mozzarella and the parmesan cheese.

5. Add the tender-crisp lid and set to bake on 400°F. Bake for about 25 to 30 minutes until hot and bubbly.

6. Serve immediately and enjoy.

Broccoli and Pesto Penne

Preparation time: 11 minutes

Cooking time: 35 minutes

Overall time: 46 minutes

Serves: 4 people

Recipe Ingredients:
- ❖ 8 ounces of whole wheat penne
- ❖ 2 cups of baby broccoli
- ❖ 1 cup of oven roasted tomatoes
- ❖ 1 teaspoons of finely chopped garlic
- ❖ ¼ cup of pesto
- ❖ ¼ cup of crumbled feta cheese
- ❖ ½ tablespoon of lemon juice
- ❖ 2 tablespoons of chopped fresh basil

Cooking Instructions:
1. Add enough water to the cooking pot to cook the pasta. Then set to sauté on high and bring to a boil.

2. Add the penne and cook according to package directions. After that, add the broccoli to the pot in the last 2 minutes of cooking time. Drain and return to the pot.

3. Reduce heat to med-high. Add tomatoes and garlic and cook for 2 minutes, stirring frequently.

4. Stir in the pesto, half the feta, and lemon juice and toss to combine. Spoon onto serving plates and top with remaining feta and basil before serving.

5. Serve immediately and enjoy

Sweet Potato Noodles with Cashew Sauce

Preparation time: 16 minutes

Cooking time: 35 minutes

Overall time: 46 minutes

Serves: 4 people

Recipe Ingredients:

- ❖ 1 cup of cashews
- ❖ ¾ cup of water
- ❖ ½ teaspoon of salt
- ❖ 1 garlic clove
- ❖ 2 tablespoons of olive oil, divided
- ❖ 4 large sweet potatoes, spiralized
- ❖ 2 cups of baby spinach
- ❖ ½ cup of chopped fresh basil

Cooking Instructions:

1. Add cashews to a small bowl and cover it with water; let soak for 2 hours.

2. After 2 hours, drain off the water, rinse, and add to a food processor with ¾ cup of water, salt, and garlic; pulse until smooth.

3. Add half the oil to the cooking pot and set to sauté on med-high heat. Add sweet potatoes and cook for 6 to 7 minutes or until tender-crisp.

4. Add spinach and toss for 1 to 2 minutes or until it wilts. Then turn off the heat and stir in half the herbs and the cashew sauce.

5. Divide evenly among serving plates, drizzle with olive oil and garnish with remaining herbs. Serve immediately.

Mushroom Goulash

Preparation time: 11 minutes

Cooking time: 40 minutes

Overall time: 51 minutes

Serves: 6 people

Recipe Ingredients:

- ❖ 2 tablespoons of olive oil (divided)
- ❖ ½ sliced thin onion
- ❖ 1 red bell pepper, chopped
- ❖ 2 pounds of chopped mushrooms
- ❖ ½ teaspoon of salt
- ❖ ¼ teaspoon of pepper
- ❖ 14 ounces of diced tomatoes
- ❖ 2 cups of low sodium vegetable broth
- ❖ 1 teaspoon of garlic powder
- ❖ 1 ½ tablespoon of paprika
- ❖ 5 to 6 sprigs fresh thyme

Cooking Instructions:

1. Add half the oil to the cooking pot and set to sauté on med-high.

2. Add the onion and cook until they start to get soft for about 4 minutes. Then add the red pepper and cook for about 3 to 5 minutes or until onions start to caramelize and transfer to a plate.

3. Add the remaining oil to the pot and let it get hot. Add the mushrooms and cook until liquid is almost evaporated while stirring occasionally. Season with salt and pepper.

4. Add the peppers and onions back to the pot along with tomatoes, broth, garlic powder, paprika, and thyme, stir to mix very well. Bring to a boil, cover, reduce heat to med-low and let cook for 20 minutes. Serve immediately.

Sour Cream and Onion Frittata

Preparation time: 16 minutes

Cooking time: 15 minutes

Overall time: 31 minutes

Serves: 3 to 6 people

Recipe Ingredients:

- ❖ 1 pounds of new potatoes (boiled peeled & sliced ¼-inch thick)
- ❖ 1 ½ tablespoons of olive oil
- ❖ 1 ½ tablespoons of butter
- ❖ 1 sliced thin onion
- ❖ 10 eggs
- ❖ ¾ cup of cheddar cheese
- ❖ ½ teaspoon of salt
- ❖ ¼ teaspoon of pepper
- ❖ ½ cup of sour cream

Cooking Instructions:

1. Start by adding oil and butter to the cooking pot and set to sauté on med-high heat.

2. Add the onions and cook for 3 to 5 minutes until soft. Add the potatoes and cook until golden brown, about 5 minutes, stirring occasionally.

3. Then in a large bowl, beat eggs, stir in cheese, salt and pepper and pour over the onion mixture.

4. Spoon sour cream over the eggs and swirl it evenly around the frittata. Reduce heat to medium and cook for about 2 to 4 minutes or until edges are set, do not stir.

5. Add the tender-crisp lid and set to bake on 400°F. Bake frittata for 10 to 12 minutes or until eggs are completely set.

6. Use a knife to loosen the edges and invert onto a cutting board. Let it cool slightly before serving. Plate, serve and enjoy.

BBQ Lentils

Preparation time: 16 minutes

Cooking time: 35 minutes

Overall time: 51 minutes

Serves: 3 to 6 people

Recipe Ingredients:

- ❖ ½ teaspoon of pepper
- ❖ ½ teaspoon of paprika
- ❖ 1/8 teaspoon of cayenne pepper
- ❖ 4 whole wheat hamburger buns
- ❖ 2 finely chopped garlic cloves
- ❖ 1 cup of dry brown lentils
- ❖ 2 ½ cups of water
- ❖ 2 tablespoons of unsweetened applesauce
- ❖ 1 tablespoon of extra virgin olive oil
- ❖ 1 finely chopped onion
- ❖ 1 finely chopped carrot
- ❖ 1 ½ teaspoons of garlic powder
- ❖ 1 ½ teaspoons of onion powder
- ❖ 1 6 ounces of tomato paste
- ❖ 3 tablespoons of apple cider vinegar
- ❖ 2 tablespoons of blackstrap molasses
- ❖ 1 teaspoon of mustard
- ❖ 1 teaspoon of salt

Cooking Instructions:

1. Add the oil to the cooking pot and set to sauté on med-high heat. Add the onion and cook for 5 minutes, stirring frequently.

2. Add the carrot and cook for another 8 minutes, or until it becomes tender. Add garlic and cook for 1 minute more.

3. After one minute, add remaining ingredients to the pot and stir to mix thoroughly well.

4. After that, add the lid and set to pressure cook on high. Set the timer for 20 minutes.

5. Once the timer goes off, use quick release to remove the pressure. Then stir very well.

6. Serve on whole wheat buns.

Curried Vegetables

Preparation time: 16 minutes

Cooking time: 10 minutes

Overall time: 26 minutes

Serves: 3 to 6 people

Recipe Ingredients:

- ❖ 1 ½ tablespoons of olive oil
- ❖ 1 ½ cups of onion, chopped
- ❖ 1 ½ tablespoons of fresh ginger, grated
- ❖ 1 ½ tablespoons of garlic, chopped fine
- ❖ 4 ½ peeled & chopped carrots,
- ❖ 1 ½ red bell peppers, (sliced in thin strips)
- ❖ 1 ½ orange bell peppers (sliced in thin strips)
- ❖ 4 cups of unsweetened coconut milk,
- ❖ 1 ½ cups of kale, ribs removed & chopped
- ❖ ¾ cup of water
- ❖ 3 tablespoons of curry powder

Cooking Instructions:

1. Start by adding oil to the cooking pot and set to sauté on med-high heat.

2. Add the onion and cook for about 3 to 4 minutes or until its translucent. Then add ginger and garlic and cook for 1 minute more.

3. Stir in carrots and bell peppers and cook for about 3 to 4 minutes or until peppers are tender

4. Stir in coconut milk, kale, water and curry paste until combined. Add the lid and set to pressure cook on high.

5. Set timer for 2 minutes. Once timer goes off, use quick release to remove the pressure.

6. Stir well and serve immediately.

Zucchini Rice Gratin

Preparation time: 16 minutes

Cooking time: 1 hr.

Overall time: 1 hr. 16 minutes

Serves: 3 to 6 people

Recipe Ingredients:

- ❖ Nonstick cooking spray
- ❖ 5 tablespoons of olive oil, divided
- ❖ 1 finely chopped onion
- ❖ 2 finely chopped garlic cloves
- ❖ ½ cup of rice
- ❖ ½ teaspoon of salt
- ❖ ¼ teaspoon of pepper
- ❖ 2 ½ pounds of trimmed & grated zucchini
- ❖ ½ cup of low sodium vegetable broth
- ❖ 2/3 cup of parmesan cheese (divided)

Cooking Instructions:

1. Spray a 2-quart of baking dish with cooking spray. After that, add 3 tablespoons of the oil to the cooking pot and set to sauté on medium heat.

2. Add the onions and cook for about 8 to 10 minutes or until translucent. Increase heat to med-high and cook until lightly browned while stirring.

3. Stir in garlic and cook for 1 minute more. Add the rice and cook, stirring for 2 minutes.

4. Season with salt and pepper. Add to zucchini in a large bowl and mix thoroughly well.

5. Stir in broth and all but 2 tablespoons of the cheese. Transfer to prepared dish and cover with foil.

6. Place the rack in the pot and place the dish on it. Add the tender-crisp lid and set to bake on 325°F.

7. Bake for 50 to 60 minutes or until rice is tender. Once rice is tender, remove foil and drizzle top with remaining oil and cheese.

8. Set to broil, broil 2 to 3 minutes or until top is golden brown and cheese is melted.

9. Serve immediately and enjoy.

Corn and Black Bean Chili

Preparation time: 16 minutes

Cooking time: 15 minutes

Overall time: 31 minutes

Serves: 3 to 6 people

Recipe Ingredients:

- ❖ 2 ½ cups of rinsed & sorted black beans
- ❖ 6 ½ cups of water
- ❖ 4 finely chopped garlic cloves
- ❖ 1 chopped red bell pepper,
- ❖ 1 chopped green bell pepper
- ❖ 2 chopped chilies in adobo sauce,
- ❖ 1 chopped red onion
- ❖ 14 ounces of diced tomatoes
- ❖ 1 tablespoon of salt
- ❖ 2 tablespoons of chili powder
- ❖ 1 tablespoon of ground cumin
- ❖ 1 tablespoon of tomato paste
- ❖ 2 cups of water
- ❖ 2 cups of corn

Cooking Instructions:

1. Add beans and water to the cooking pot. Add the lid and set to pressure cook on high.

2. Set the timer for 8 minutes. Once timer goes off, use quick release to remove the pressure then drain beans and return to pot.

3. Add remaining ingredients, except the corn, and stir to mix. Recover and pressure cook on high.

4. Set the timer for 4 minutes. Once the timer goes off, use quick release to remove the pressure again. Stir in the corn and pressure cook for another 2 to 3 minutes. Stir well and serve immediately.

Caramelized Sweet Potatoes

Preparation time: 6 minutes

Cooking time: 20 minutes

Overall time: 26 minutes

Serves: 2 to 4 people

Recipe Ingredients:

- ❖ 1 cup of water

- ❖ 2 large sweet potatoes

- ❖ 2 tablespoons of butter

- ❖ ½ teaspoon of salt

- ❖ ¼ teaspoon of pepper

Cooking Instructions:

1. Add the trivet and water to the cooking pot. Pierce the potatoes with a fork and place on the trivet. Then add the lid and set to pressure cook on high.

2. Set timer for 15 minutes. Once timer goes off, use natural release to remove the pressure.

3. Transfer potatoes to a cutting board and slice ½-inch thick. After that, remove the trivet and add butter to the pot. Set to sauté on med-high heat.

4. Add the potatoes and cook, turning occasionally, until potatoes are nicely browned on both sides.

5. Season with salt and pepper and serve to enjoy.

Southern Veggie Bake

Preparation time: 16 minutes

Cooking time: 30 minutes

Overall time: 46 minutes

Serves: 5 to 10 people

Recipe Ingredients:
- ❖ Nonstick cooking spray
- ❖ 1 sliced thin onion
- ❖ 1 sliced thin green bell pepper
- ❖ 1 sliced thin red bell pepper
- ❖ 2 sliced thin lengthwise zucchini
- ❖ 2 yellow squash, sliced thin lengthwise
- ❖ ½ cup of grated sharp cheddar cheese, (reduced fat)
- ❖ 8 ounces of fat free sour cream
- ❖ 10 ¾ ounce of low-fat cream of celery soup
- ❖ 1 cup of crushed crackers,
- ❖ 1 tablespoon of paprika
- ❖ 1 teaspoon of salt
- ❖ ½ teaspoon of pepper

Cooking Instructions:
1. Add the rack to the cooking pot. Spray an 8-inch casserole dish with cooking spray.

2. Layer the vegetables in the prepared dish. Then combine cheese, sour cream, and soup in a large bowl, and mix very well.

3. Spoon over the vegetables and flip to coat the vegetables. In a small bowl, combine crackers, paprika, salt, and pepper and mix well.

4. Sprinkle over the top of the vegetables. Place the dish on the rack and add the tender-crisp lid.

5. Set to bake on 375°F. Bake for 30 minutes until the top is golden brown and vegetables are tender. Serve immediately and enjoy.

Cheesy Corn Pudding

Preparation time: 11 minutes

Cooking time: 3 hrs.

Overall time: 3 hrs. 11 minutes

Serves: 3 to 6 people

Recipe Ingredients:

- ❖ 10 ounces of corn (thawed & divided)
- ❖ 1 cup of milk
- ❖ 2 tablespoons of flour
- ❖ ½ teaspoon of cumin
- ❖ 1 teaspoon of salt
- ❖ ¼ teaspoon of pepper
- ❖ 3 lightly beaten eggs,
- ❖ 2 cups of grated monterey Jack cheese
- ❖ 1 seeded & finely chopped jalapeno pepper

Cooking Instructions

1. Add ¾ cup corn, milk, flour, cumin, salt, and pepper to a food processor or blender, then pulse until it becomes smooth.

2. Spray the cooking pot with cooking spray. Pour the corn mixture into the pot then stir in remaining ingredients until combined.

3. Add the lid and set to slow cook on low. Cook for 3 hours or until pudding is set.

4. Serve hot. Delicious!

Rustic Veggie Tart

Preparation time: 20 minutes

Cooking time: 40 minutes

Overall time: 60 minutes

Serves: 3 to 6 people

Recipe Ingredients:

- ❖ 1 tablespoon of olive oil
- ❖ 3 cups of cherry tomatoes
- ❖ ½ teaspoon of salt, divided
- ❖ 1/8 teaspoon of red pepper flakes
- ❖ 1 cup of fresh corn kernels
- ❖ 1 chopped zucchini
- ❖ 5 to 6 sliced thin green onions,
- ❖ 1 ¼ cups of flour
- ❖ 8 tablespoons of sliced butter
- ❖ ¼ cup of sour cream
- ❖ 2 teaspoons of fresh lemon juice
- ❖ ¼ cup ice water
- ❖ ½ cup of parmesan cheese
- ❖ 1 egg yolk
- ❖ 1 teaspoon of water

Cooking Instructions

1. In a large bowl, combine flour and ¼ tsp salt. Cut in butter until the mixture look like coarse crumbs.

2. Again, in a small bowl, whisk together sour cream, lemon juice, and water until combined. Add to flour mixture and stir until it forms a soft dough.

3. Form dough into a ball and wrap with plastic wrap, refrigerate at least 1 hour. Add oil to the cooking pot and set to sauté on med-high heat.

4. Add tomatoes, remaining salt, and red pepper flakes, cover and cook until tomatoes burst, turning tomatoes frequently.

5. Reduce heat to medium and add zucchini. Cook for 2 minutes or until they are softened.

6. Add corn and cook for 1 minute more. Stir in scallions and turn off the heat. Transfer to a large plate and let cool.

7. Wipe out the cooking pot and add the rack. Then on a floured surface, roll out dough to a 12-inch circle. Transfer to a piece of parchment paper.

8. Sprinkle vegetables with half the parmesan cheese and spoon into the center of the dough, leaving a 2-inch border.

9. Sprinkle most of the remaining parmesan over the vegetables. Fold edges over the filling, pleating as you go.

10. In a small bowl, beat together egg yolk and teaspoon of water and brush the crust with egg yolk glaze and sprinkle with the last of the parmesan.

11. Carefully pick up the parchment paper and transfer to the rack in the cooking pot.

12. Add the tender-crisp lid and set to bake on 400°F. Bake 30 to 40 minutes until golden brown.

13. Transfer to wire rack to cool for 5 minutes before serving.

14. Serve and enjoy your delicious meal.

Artichoke and Spinach Casserole

Preparation time: 11 minutes

Cooking time: 30 minutes

Overall time: 41 minutes

Serves: 3 to 6 people

Recipe Ingredients:

- ❖ Nonstick cooking spray
- ❖ 2 teaspoons of olive oil
- ❖ ½ cup of chopped onion,
- ❖ 3 finely chopped garlic cloves
- ❖ 1 cup quinoa cooked
- ❖ 14 ounces of artichoke hearts, drained & chopped
- ❖ 10 ounces of spinach, thawed & chopped
- ❖ ¾ cup of mozzarella cheese, grated, divided
- ❖ ½ teaspoon of nutmeg
- ❖ ¼ teaspoon of pepper
- ❖ 2 eggs
- ❖ ¾ cup of plain Greek yogurt

Cooking Instructions:

1. Spray cooking pot with cooking spray and add oil and set to sauté on medium heat.

2. Add onion and garlic and cook for 3 to 5 minutes, stirring frequently, until onion is soft the turn off heat.

3. In a large bowl, combine quinoa, artichokes, spinach, ½ cup mozzarella, nutmeg, and pepper, mix very well.

4. In a medium bowl, whisk together egg and yogurt and stir into quinoa mixture. Sprinkle remaining cheese over the top.

5. Add the tender-crisp lid and set to bake on 375°F. Bake 25 to 30 minutes until heated through and cheese is melted and starting to brown. Serve immediately and enjoy.

CHAPTER 6 - RICE GRAINS & PASTA RECIPES
Green Chili Mac N Cheese

Preparation time: 21 minutes

Cooking time: 45 minutes

Overall time: 1 hr. 6 minutes

Serves: 3 to 6 people

Recipe Ingredients:

- ❖ Nonstick cooking spray

- ❖ 6 Anaheim chilies

- ❖ 3 tablespoons of unsalted butter
- ❖ 3 tablespoons of flour
- ❖ 2 cups of milk
- ❖ 1 cup of grated fine jack cheese

- ❖ 1 cup of grated fine sharp cheddar cheese

- ❖ 2 cups of directs drained elbow macaroni (cooked 2 minutes less than pkg.)

- ❖ 1 cup of corn kernels

- ❖ 1 tablespoon of lime juice

- ❖ 1 teaspoon of salt

- ❖ ¼ cup of panko bread crumbs

Cooking Instructions:

1. Spray the fryer basket with cooking spray; place the chilies in the basket and add the tender-crisp lid and set to broil.

2. Cook until charred on all sides, then transfer to a bowl and cover with plastic wrap. Let it sit for 10 minutes, remove skin, seeds, and stems and chop.

3. Add the butter to the cooking pot and set to sauté on medium heat. Once the butter has melted, whisk in flour until smooth. Cook for about 2 minutes, stirring frequently,

4. Slowly whisk in the milk, a little at a time, until it is smooth. Stir in cheeses, 1/3 at a time, stirring after each addition.

5. Stir in macaroni, chilies, corn, and lime juice until it is combined. Season with salt and sprinkle the bread crumbs over the top.

6. Add the tender-crisp lid and set to bake on 400°F. Bake for 25 to 30 minutes until top is lightly browned. Let it sit 10 minutes before serving.

Simple Spanish Rice

Preparation time: 6 minutes

Cooking time: 20 minutes

Overall time: 26 minutes

Serves: 3 to 6 people

Recipe Ingredients:

- ❖ 1 tablespoon of extra-virgin olive oil
- ❖ 1 tablespoon of butter
- ❖ 1 cup of white rice
- ❖ 1 cup of low sodium chicken broth
- ❖ 1 cup of tomato sauce
- ❖ 1 ½ teaspoons of chili powder
- ❖ 1 teaspoon of cumin
- ❖ ½ teaspoon of garlic salt
- ❖ ½ teaspoon of oregano
- ❖ ¼ cup of seeded & chopped tomatoes

Cooking Instructions:

1. Add the oil and butter to the cooking pot and set to sauté on medium heat.

2. Once the butter has melted, add the rice and cook for about 2 to 3 minutes, stirring frequently.

3. Stir in remaining ingredients and mix well. Increase heat and bring to a boil, stirring occasionally.

4. Once mixture begins to boil, cover, reduce heat to low, and cook for 20 minutes until rice is tender and liquid is absorbed.

5. Turn off heat and let it sit 3 to 5 minutes. Remove lid, fluff with a fork and serve immediately.

Irish Brown Bread

Preparation time: 6 minutes

Cooking time: 40 minutes

Overall time: 46 minutes

Serves: 16 people

Recipe Ingredients:

- ❖ 1 ½ cups of whole wheat flour
- ❖ Nonstick cooking spray
- ❖ 1 cup of flour
- ❖ 1 egg
- ❖ 1 cup of buttermilk, low fat
- ❖ 1 teaspoon of baking soda
- ❖ 1 teaspoon of salt
- ❖ 2 tablespoons of light butter (cut in small pieces)

Cooking Instructions:

1. Spray a small baking sheet with cooking spray and place the rack in the cooking pot.

2. In a large bowl, mix both flours, baking soda, and salt and stir to mix well. After that, add butter, egg, and buttermilk.

3. Use your hands to mix just until ingredients are combined. Place dough on the prepared pan and shape into a round loaf 1-inch high.

4. Use a floured knife to score an X on the top of the loaf. Place the pan on the rack.

5. Add the tender-crisp lid and set to bake on 425°F. Bake for 10 minutes. Reduce temperature to 350°F and bake for 25 to 30 minutes or until bread passes the toothpick test.

6. Transfer to a wire rack to cool. To serve, cut in wedges and serve warm. Delicious!

Coconut Bread

Preparation time: 6 minutes

Cooking time: 1 hr. 15 minutes

Overall time: 1 hr. 21 minutes

Serves: 10 people

Recipe Ingredients:
- ❖ Nonstick cooking spray
- ❖ 2 eggs
- ❖ 1 ¼ cups of milk
- ❖ 1 teaspoon of vanilla
- ❖ 2 ½ cups of flour
- ❖ ¼ teaspoon of salt
- ❖ 2 teaspoons of baking powder
- ❖ 2 teaspoons of cinnamon
- ❖ 1 cup of sugar
- ❖ 1 ½ cups of coconut
- ❖ 6 tablespoons of melted unsalted butter,

Cooking Instructions:
1. Place the rack in the cooking pot and spray a loaf pan with cooking spray. Then in a small bowl, whisk together eggs, milk, and vanilla until it is smooth.

2. In a medium bowl, stir together flour, salt, baking powder, and cinnamon until it is combined. Add sugar and coconut and mix well.

3. Make a well in the center of the dry ingredients and pour in egg mixture. Stir thoroughly until ingredients are combined.

4. Add butter and stir until smooth, pour into prepared pan. Place the pan on the rack and add the tender-crisp lid.

5. Set to bake on 350°F. Bake for 60 to 75 minutes, or until bread passes the toothpick test then remove from cooking pot.

6. Let bread cool in pan for 5 minutes, then invert onto wire rack and cool completely. Serve and enjoy immediately.

Asian Sticky Rice

Preparation time: 6 minutes

Cooking time: 5 minutes

Overall time: 11 minutes

Serves: 3 to 6 people
Recipe Ingredients:
- ❖ 3 cups of water
- ❖ 3 cups of Jasmine Rice
- ❖ 1 tablespoon of sesame oil
- ❖ 2 tablespoons of rice vinegar

Cooking Instructions:

1. Add the water, rice, and oil to the cooking pot and stir thoroughly well to mix.

2. Add the lid and set to pressure cook on high. Set the timer for 4 minutes. When the timer goes off, use manual release to remove the pressure.

3. Add the vinegar and fluff rice with a large spoon. Once food is ready serve immediately and enjoy.

Mushroom Risotto

Preparation time: 11 minutes

Cooking time: 45 minutes

Overall time: 56 minutes

Serves: 3 to 6 people

Recipe Ingredients:

- ❖ 5 ½ cups of chicken broth, low sodium
- ❖ 2 tablespoons of butter
- ❖ 2 cups of chanterelle mushrooms (sliced ½-inch thick)
- ❖ 1/3 cup of finely chopped shallots
- ❖ 1 ¾ cups of Arborio rice
- ❖ 2/3 cup of brandy
- ❖ 1/3 cup of grated fresh parmesan cheese
- ❖ ½ teaspoon of salt
- ❖ ¼ teaspoon of pepper
- ❖ 2 tablespoons of chopped chives,

Cooking Instructions:

1. Add the broth to a small saucepan and bring it to a cook over medium heat.

2. Add the butter to the cooking pot and set to sauté on med-high heat. Once it melts, add the mushrooms and shallots and cook for 5 minutes, stirring occasionally.

3. Stir in the rice and brandy, bring to a boil and let cook for about 3 to 4 minutes until liquid has reduced by half.

4. Pour in the simmering broth, half at a time, stirring constantly. Skim off the starch as needed.

5. Pour the second half of the broth in when the first half is almost completely absorbed. This step should take about 25 minutes.

6. Stir in parmesan and season with salt and pepper. Scoop onto plates or into bowls and garnish with chives. Serve immediately.

Lemon Spaghetti

Preparation time: 6 minutes

Cooking time: 15 minutes

Overall time: 21 minutes

Serves: 3 to 6 people
Recipe Ingredients:
- ❖ 1 pound of spaghetti
- ❖ ¼ cup of olive oil
- ❖ ¼ cup of heavy cream
- ❖ 3 lemons juiced & zested
- ❖ ½ cup of grated parmesan cheese
- ❖ ¼ cup of chopped arugula
- ❖ 1 teaspoon of salt
- ❖ ½ teaspoon of pepper

Cooking Instructions:

1. Fill the cooking pot with well-salted water and set to sauté on high heat. Then cook the spaghetti according to package directions.

2. Drain, reserving 1 ½ cups of the pasta water. Add the oil, cream, zest, and 1 cup of the pasta water and bring to a boil. Cook for 2 minutes, stirring occasionally.

3. Return the pasta to the pot and stir to coat. Stir in the cheese, and ½ the lemon juice and toss well to mix everything together.

4. Depending on how loose you like your pasta, you can add more pasta water if you like.

5. Stir in arugula, salt, and pepper. Taste and adjust seasonings to your liking. Scoop onto plates and drizzle with a little more olive oil and parmesan cheese.

6. Serve immediately.

Honey Whole Wheat Cornbread

Preparation time: 11 minutes

Cooking time: 25 minutes

Overall time: 36 minutes

Serves: 3 to 6 people

Recipe Ingredients:

- ❖ Butter flavored cooking spray
- ❖ 1 cup of yellow cornmeal
- ❖ 1/3 cup of whole wheat flour
- ❖ 1/3 cup of flour
- ❖ 1 tablespoon of baking powder
- ❖ 1 ½ teaspoon of salt
- ❖ 1 cup of sour cream
- ❖ ½ cup of milk
- ❖ 1/3 cup of honey
- ❖ 2 eggs
- ❖ ¼ teaspoon of baking soda
- ❖ 1 stick unsalted butter

Cooking Instructions:

1. Place the rack in the cooking pot. Spray an 8-inch cake pan with cooking spray.

2. In a large bowl, whisk together cornmeal, flours, baking powder, and salt, mix well.

3. In a separate bowl, combine sour cream, milk, honey, eggs, and baking soda, mix well.

4. Fold the wet ingredients into the dry and stir just until combined. Stir in melted butter and pour into prepared pan.

5. Place the pan on the rack and add the tender-crisp lid. Set to bake on 375°F. Bake for 25 minutes or until cornbread passes the toothpick test.

6. Transfer to a wire rack and cool slightly before serving.

Quick Quinoa Risotto

Preparation time: 6 minutes

Cooking time: 10 minutes

Overall time: 16 minutes

Serves: 2 to 4 people

Recipe Ingredients:

- ❖ 1 cup of spaghetti sauce
- ❖ ¼ cup of low sodium vegetable broth,
- ❖ 4 cups of cooked quinoa
- ❖ ¼ cup of grated pecorino Romano cheese,
- ❖ 2 tablespoons of chopped fresh parsle,

Cooking Instructions:

1. Add the spaghetti sauce and broth to the cooking pot and set to saute on medium heat.

2. Cook for about 2 to 3 minutes while stirring occasionally or until it heated through.

3. Stir in quinoa and cheese and mix well. Spoon onto plates and top with parsley.

4. Serve immediately.

Savory English Muffins

Preparation time: 10 minutes

Cooking time: 25 minutes

Overall time: 35 minutes

Serves: 2 to 4 people

Recipe Ingredients:

- ❖ 2 eggs
- ❖ ¼ teaspoon of garlic powder
- ❖ ¼ teaspoon of onion powder
- ❖ 1/8 teaspoon of salt
- ❖ Nonstick cooking spray
- ❖ 2 ounces of soft cream cheese
- ❖ 2 tablespoons of soft butter,
- ❖ 2 tablespoons of coconut flour
- ❖ 2 tablespoon of parmesan cheese
- ❖ ½ teaspoon of baking powder
- ❖ ¼ teaspoon of Italian seasoning

Cooking Instructions:

1. Place the trivet in the cooking pot and spray 21-cups of glass baking dishes with cooking spray.

2. In a large bowl, beat together cream cheese, butter, and eggs until smooth.

3. Beat in remaining ingredients until it's combined. Divide mixture evenly between the prepared dishes. And cover tightly with foil.

4. Pour water into the cooking pot. Place the dishes on the trivet. Add the lid and set to pressure cook on high.

5. Set the timer for 20 minutes. When the timer goes off, use quick release to remove the pressure.

6. Carefully remove the muffins from the cooking pot and cool completely. Slice in half horizontally and toast or broil to brown them. Serve immediately.

Mushroom Garlic Quinoa

Preparation time: 6 minutes

Cooking time: 10 minutes

Overall time: 16 minutes

Serves: 3 to 6 people

Recipe Ingredients:

- ❖ 1 tablespoon of olive oil
- ❖ 1 pound of sliced thin cremini mushrooms
- ❖ 5 chopped fine garlic cloves
- ❖ ½ teaspoon of thyme
- ❖ ½ teaspoon of salt
- ❖ ¼ teaspoon of pepper
- ❖ 1 cup of cooked quinoa
- ❖ 2 tablespoons of parmesan cheese

Cooking Instructions:

1. Add oil to the cooking pot and set to sauté on med-high heat.

2. Add mushrooms, garlic, and thyme and cook, stirring occasionally, about 3 to 4 minutes or until mushrooms are tender.

3. Season with salt and pepper. Add quinoa and mix well. Cook 2 to 3 minutes or until it is heated through.

4. Spoon on to serving plates and top with parmesan cheese.

5. Serve immediately.

Mexican Quinoa

Preparation time: 6 minutes

Cooking time: 10 minutes

Overall time: 16 minutes

Serves: 3 to 6 people

Recipe Ingredients:

- ❖ Nonstick cooking spray
- ❖ 1 cup of fresh corn kernels
- ❖ 15 ounces of black beans, drained & rinsed
- ❖ 3 cups white quinoa, cooked
- ❖ 1 tablespoon of cumin
- ❖ 1 cup of salsa
- ❖ ¼ cup of chopped cilantro

Cooking Instructions:

1. Spray cooking pot with cooking spray and set to sauté on medium heat. Add corn and black beans and cook for about 3 minutes or until corn is tender.

2. Stir in quinoa and cumin and mix well. Cook for about 3 minutes, until quinoa starts to get a little crunchy while stirring constantly.

3. Stir in salsa and cook for another 2 minutes until it is heated through and liquid reduces.

4. Turn off heat and let it sit for 5 to 10 minutes. Fluff with a fork and serve garnished with cilantro. Enjoy your meal.

Bacon and Sage Polenta

Preparation time: 6 minutes

Cooking time: 30 minutes

Overall time: 36 minutes

Serves: 5 people

Recipe Ingredients:

- ❖ 4 slices of chopped bacon,
- ❖ 1 tablespoon of chopped fresh sage,
- ❖ 1 cup of corn
- ❖ 4 cups of water
- ❖ 1 cup of polenta
- ❖ ½ teaspoon of salt
- ❖ ¼ teaspoon of pepper
- ❖ ½ cup of parmesan cheese

Cooking Instructions:

1. Add bacon to the cooking pot and set to sauté on med-high heat. Cook until it becomes crisp.

2. Use a slotted spoon to transfer to paper towel lined plate. Drain all but 1 tablespoon of the fat.

3. Add sage and corn and cook for 1 minute. Pour in water and bring to a boil. Slowly whisk in polenta.

4. Reduce heat to low and cook for about 20 minutes or until polenta starts to thicken, stirring frequently - for traditional polenta.

5. If mixture becomes too thick stir in more water. After that, season with salt and pepper. Stir in cheese and bacon and serve immediately.

Quinoa Succotash

Preparation time: 10 minutes

Cooking time: 30 minutes

Overall time: 40 minutes

Serves: 2 to 4 people

Recipe Ingredients:

- ❖ 1 slice bacon, thick cut, halved

- ❖ ½ cup of chopped onion

- ❖ 2 tablespoons of butter

- ❖ 1 cup of quinoa

- ❖ 1 cup of corn

- ❖ ½ cup of baby lima beans

- ❖ ½ cup of chopped fresh tomatoes

- ❖ ½ teaspoon of thyme

- ❖ ½ cup + 2 tablespoons of water

- ❖ 1 cup of low sodium chicken broth

- ❖ ½ teaspoon of salt

- ❖ 2 teaspoons of lemon juice

- ❖ ¼ cup of chopped green onions

Cooking Instructions:

1. Add the bacon to the cooking pot and set to sauté on medium heat. Cook until fat renders and bacon is lightly browned.

2. Use a slotted spoon to transfer it to a paper towel lined plate once it cools enough to handle, chop.

3. Add the onion along with the butter and cook for 3 to 4 minutes until onions are translucent.

4. Add the quinoa and increase heat to med-high. Stir well and let cook 2 to 3 minutes.

5. Add the corn, lima beans, tomato, bacon, and thyme and stir to mix. Add the water and broth and increase heat to high and bring to a boil.

6. Add the lid and set to pressure cook on high. Set timer for 8 minutes. When timer goes off, use natural release to remove the pressure.

7. Stir in lemon juice and green onions and serve immediately.

Linguine with Pea Pesto

Preparation time: 6 minutes

Cooking time: 5 minutes

Overall time: 11 minutes

Serves: 2 to 4 people

Recipe Ingredients:

- ❖ 1 ½ cups of thawed peas
- ❖ 12 ounces of linguine
- ❖ 1 chopped fine garlic clove
- ❖ 2 tablespoons of toasted and cooled pine nuts,
- ❖ ½ cup of parmesan cheese
- ❖ ¼ teaspoon of salt
- ❖ 1/3 cup of olive oil

Cooking Instructions:

1. Add a cup of water to the pot, set to sauté on high heat and bring to a boil. Cook the peas for 2 minutes and drain well and let cool slightly.

2. Fill the cooking pot with salted water and bring to a boil, cook pasta according to package directions the, drain, reserving 2 cups of pasta water.

3. Reserve ½ cup of the peas. Place the remaining peas with the garlic, pine nuts, 1/3 cup parmesan, and salt in a food processor.

4. Process until smooth, scraping down sides as needed. With machine running, slowly add oil and set aside.

5. Then return the pasta to the pot and decrease heat to medium and add the pea pesto and peas; toss to combine well.

6. Add enough water to smooth out the pesto to desired consistency. Let it cook for 1 minute.

7. Taste and adjust seasonings as needed. Serve immediately garnished with remaining parmesan cheese. Enjoy!

Classic Polenta

Preparation time: 6 minutes

Cooking time: 3 hrs.

Overall time: 3 hrs. 6 minutes

Serves: 2 to 4 people

Recipe Ingredients:
- ❖ 1 cup of polenta
- ❖ 5 cups of water
- ❖ ½ teaspoon of salt
- ❖ 1 cup of parmesan cheese

Cooking Instructions:

1. Start by adding the polenta, water, and salt to the cooking pot, stir well to combine.

2. After that, add the lid and set to slow cook on high and cook for 2 good hours.

3. Remove the lid and stir well. Add more water if it seems too thick. then Recover and cook for 1 hour more.

4. Stir in the parmesan cheese and serve hot.

Pumpkin Polenta

Preparation time: 6 minutes

Cooking time: 35 minutes

Overall time: 41 minutes

Serves: 3 to 6 people

Recipe Ingredients:

- ❖ 2 cups of pumpkin
- ❖ 2 ½ cups of milk
- ❖ ¼ cup of heavy cream
- ❖ 1 teaspoon of rosemary
- ❖ 1 teaspoon of thyme
- ❖ ½ teaspoon of salt
- ❖ ¼ teaspoon of pepper
- ❖ 1 cup of polenta
- ❖ ¼ cup of parmesan cheese
- ❖ 2 tablespoons of butter

Cooking Instructions:

1. Add the pumpkin, milk, and cream to the cooking pot, stir to mix. Set to sauté on med-low heat and bring to a low boil.

2. Stir in rosemary, thyme, salt and pepper, mix well. Whisk in polenta and cook, stirring frequently, until it thicken for about 25 to 30 minutes.

3. Stir in the parmesan cheese and butter until butter has melted.

4. Serve warm immediately and enjoy.

Spinach and Mushroom "Rice"

Preparation time: 11 minutes

Cooking time: 15 minutes

Overall time: 31 minutes

Serves: 2 to 4 people

Recipe Ingredients:

- ❖ 1 tablespoon of olive oil
- ❖ 2 cups of grated cauliflower
- ❖ ½ cup of chopped onion
- ❖ 3 cups of sliced mushrooms
- ❖ 2 finely chopped garlic cloves
- ❖ 1 tablespoon of soy sauce
- ❖ 2 cups spinach

Cooking Instructions:

1. Start by adding oil to the cooking pot and set to sauté on medium heat.

2. Add the cauliflower and onion and cook for about 3 to 5 minutes, stirring frequently until onion is soft.

3. Stir in mushrooms and cook until tender, for about 3 to 5 minutes and most of the liquid has been absorbed. Stir in the garlic and cook 1 minute more.

4. Stir in the soy sauce and cook about 1 minute until it is absorbed by the cauliflower.

5. Add the spinach and cook until wilted for about 2 minutes. Serve immediately.

Baked Brown Rice

Preparation time: 6 minutes

Cooking time: 1 hr. 10 minutes

Overall time: 1 hr. 16 minutes

Serves: 2 to 4 people

Recipe Ingredients:
- ½ teaspoon of salt
- ¼ teaspoon of pepper
- 1 tablespoon of olive oil
- 1 chopped fine onion
- 3 chopped fine cloves garlic
- 3 ¼ cups of water
- 1½ cups of long grain brown rice
- 2 tablespoons of chopped fresh parsley

Cooking Instructions:
1. Add the oil to the cooking pot and set to sauté on medium heat.

2. Add onion and cook for 10 minutes, stirring occasionally, until onions are golden brown. Stir in garlic and cook for 1 minute more.

3. Add the water and increase the heat to med-high. Bring to a boil and stir in rice and turn off heat.

4. Add the tender-crisp lid and set to bake on 375°F. Bake for 60 minutes or until rice is cooked through and liquid is absorbed.

5. Fluff with a fork, Stir in parsley, salt and pepper and serve immediately.

Parmesan Garlic Noodles

Preparation time: 11 minutes

Cooking time: 20 minutes

Overall time: 31 minutes

Serves: 2 to 4 people

Recipe Ingredients:

❖ 10 tablespoons of butter

❖ 3 finely chopped garlic cloves,

❖ 1 teaspoon of red pepper flakes

❖ 8 ounces of cooked & drained spaghetti,

❖ ½ cup of parmesan cheese

❖ ½ teaspoon of salt

❖ ¼ teaspoon of pepper

❖ 2 tablespoons of chopped fresh parsley

Cooking Instructions:

1. Add butter, garlic, and pepper flakes to the cooking pot. Set to sauté on medium heat and cook until butter has melted.

2. Cook, whisking constantly, until butter begins to turn a golden brown for about 4 to 5 minutes.

3. Turn off heat and stir in pasta and parmesan, mix well. Season with salt and pepper and serve garnished with parsley.

4. Enjoy very delicious!

Fried Rice

Preparation time: 16 minutes

Cooking time: 8 minutes

Overall time: 24 minutes

Serves: 2 to 4 people

Recipe Ingredients:

- ❖ 1 cup of rice
- ❖ 1 cup of chicken broth, low sodium
- ❖ 1 chopped onion
- ❖ ½ cup of peas & carrots, frozen
- ❖ 1 tablespoon of olive oil
- ❖ 1 lightly beaten egg
- ❖ 3 tablespoons of tamari
- ❖ 2 sliced green onions

Cooking Instructions:

1. Start by adding the rice, broth, onion, and vegetables to the cooking pot, stir to mix.

2. Add the lid and set to pressure cook on high. Set the timer for 8 minutes. When the timer goes off, use quick release to remove the pressure.

3. Stir the rice and create a well in the center. Add oil and set to sauté on med-high.

4. Add the egg to the middle and cook to scramble. Stir the egg into the rice. Add the tamari and serve garnished with green onions.

5. Serve immediately.

Sandwich Bread

Preparation time: 11 minutes

Cooking time: 15 minutes

Overall time: 26 minutes

Serves: 3 to 6 people
Ingredients:
- ❖ 6 eggs, separated
- ❖ ¼ teaspoon of cream of tartar
- ❖ 4 tablespoons of melted butter
- ❖ 1 ½ cup of sifted almond flour
- ❖ 3 teaspoon of baking powder
- ❖ 1/8 teaspoon of salt

Cooking Instructions:
1. Add the rack to the cooking pot and spray an 8-inch loaf pan with cooking spray.

2. In a medium bowl, beat egg whites and cream of tartar until soft peaks form.

3. In a large bowl, combine egg yolks, 1/3 of beaten egg whites, butter, almond flour, baking powder, and salt and mix well.

4. Fold in remaining egg whites until combined. Pour into prepared pan.

5. Place the pan on the rack and add the tender-crisp lid. Set to bake on 375°F. Bake 25 to 30 minutes until bread passes the toothpick test.

6. Remove from the pot and let cool in the pan 10 minutes, then invert onto a wire rack to cool completely.

7. Serve immediately

Peasant Bread

Preparation time: 25 minutes

Cooking time: 2 hrs. 30 minutes

Overall time: 2 hrs. 55 minutes

Serves: 16 people

Recipe Ingredients:

- ❖ 1 ¼ cups of warm water
- ❖ 1 tablespoon of active dry yeast
- ❖ 1 teaspoon of sugar
- ❖ ½ cup of plain yogurt (at room temperature)
- ❖ ¼ cup of warm milk
- ❖ 2 ½ teaspoons of salt
- ❖ 3 ¾ cups of flour
- ❖ ¼ cup of whole wheat flour
- ❖ Nonstick cooking spray
- ❖ 1 tablespoon of yellow cornmeal

Cooking Instructions:

1. In a large bowl, stir together water, yeast, and sugar until combined and let it rest for 10 minutes until it gets foamy.

2. Stir in yogurt, milk, and salt until it's combined then in a medium bowl, stir together both flours.

3. Add 2 ½ cups of the flour to the yeast mixture and stir just until combined. Cover bowl plastic wrap and let it rise for 2 hours.

4. Stir 1¼ cups of flour into the dough; use the remaining flour to cover a work surface.

5. Place dough on the floured surface and knead for about 2 to 3 minutes or until the flour is incorporated. Cover and let it stand for another 30 minutes.

6. After 30 minutes, spray the cooking pot with cooking spray and line the bottom with parchment paper and spray it with cooking spray.

7. Sprinkle the cornmeal evenly on the bottom of the pot. Dust the top of the dough with a little flour and place in the cooking pot, keeping it shaped in a loose circle.

8. Add the lid and set to slow cook on high. Cook for about 2 ¼ to 2 ½ hours. After that, add the tender-crisp lid and set to broil.

9. Cook the bread for another 2 to 3 minutes or until it is golden brown and crusty. Transfer to a wire rack to cool completely.

10. Serve immediately and enjoy

CHAPTER 7 – SNACKS, APPETIZERS AND SIDES

Cheesy Onion Dip

Preparation time: 11 minutes

Cooking time: 15 minutes

Overall time: 26 minutes

Serves: 8 people

Recipe Ingredients:

- ❖ 8 ounces of soft cream cheese
- ❖ 1 cup of grated swiss cheese
- ❖ 1 cup of mayonnaise
- ❖ 1 cup of grated onion

Cooking Instructions:

1. In a medium bowl, combine all ingredients and mix thoroughly. Transfer to a small baking dish and cover tightly with foil.

2. Place the trivet in the cooking pot along with 1 cup of water. Place the dish on trivet.

3. Secure the lid and select pressure cooking on high then set timer for 15 minutes.

4. When timer goes off, use quick release to remove the lid.

5. Remove the foil and add the tender-crisp lid. Set to air-fryer on 400°F and cook for about 1 to 2 minutes until the top is golden brown.

6. Serve warm immediately.

Chocolate Chip and Zucchini Snack Bars

Preparation time: 11 minutes

Cooking time: 30 minutes

Overall time: 41 minutes

Serves: 12 people

Recipe Ingredients:

- ❖ Nonstick cooking spray
- ❖ 1 ¼ cup of oat flour
- ❖ ¼ cup + 2 tablespoons of coconut flour
- ❖ ¼ cup of oats
- ❖ 1 ½ teaspoons of baking powder
- ❖ ½ teaspoons of baking soda
- ❖ ½ teaspoon of cinnamon
- ❖ ¼ teaspoon of salt
- ❖ 2 mashed bananas
- ❖ 1 cup of grated zucchini,
- ❖ ½ cup of unsweetened almond milk
- ❖ ¼ cup of unsweetened applesauce
- ❖ 2 teaspoons of vanilla
- ❖ ¾ cup of chocolate chips, sugar free

Cooking Instructions:

1. Set to air-fryer on 350°F. Lightly spray an 8-inch square baking pan with cooking spray.

2. In a large bowl, combine flours, oats, baking powder, baking soda, cinnamon, and salt.

3. In a medium bowl, whisk together bananas, zucchini, milk, applesauce, and vanilla, add to dry ingredients and mix just until it is thoroughly combined.

4. Fold in chocolate chips and pour into prepared pan. Add the rack to the cooking pot and place the pan on it.

5. Add the tender-crisp lid and bake for 30 to 35 minutes or until toothpick inserted in center comes out clean.

6. Let it cool in pan for a total period of 10 minutes then cut it exactly into 12 bars.

7. Preheat oven to 350F, then lightly grease a 9×9 baking pan with cooking spray or oil.

8. Once done, serve immediately and enjoy.

Zesty Meatballs

Preparation time: 11 minutes

Cooking time: 15 minutes

Overall time: 26 minutes

Serves: 12 people

Recipe Ingredients:

- ❖ Nonstick cooking spray
- ❖ 1 pound of ground pork
- ❖ ½ cup of plain bread crumbs
- ❖ ¼ cup of water
- ❖ 1 chopped onion
- ❖ ¼ cup of chopped fresh parsley
- ❖ 1 teaspoon of crushed fennel seed
- ❖ ½ teaspoon of garlic powder
- ❖ ¼ teaspoon of cayenne pepper
- ❖ ½ teaspoon of salt
- ❖ ½ teaspoon of black pepper

Cooking Instructions:

1. Set to air-fryer on 350°F. Lightly spray fryer basket with cooking spray and put in the cooking pot.

2. In a large bowl, combine all ingredients thoroughly and form into 1-inch balls.

3. Place meatballs in a single layer in the fryer basket, these will need to be cooked in batches.

4. Add the tender-crisp lid and bake for 15 minutes, or until it is no longer pink.

5. Turn meatballs over halfway through cooking time. Once done, transfer to serving plate and enjoy.

Hot Crab Dip

Preparation time: 6 minutes

Cooking time: 30 minutes

Overall time: 36 minutes

Serves: 8 people

Recipe Instructions

- ❖ 8 ounces of cream cheese fat free, soft
- ❖ ¼ pound of flaked crabmeat,
- ❖ ½ teaspoon of fresh lemon juice
- ❖ ½ teaspoon of onion powder
- ❖ 1 tablespoon of chopped fresh dill,
- ❖ ¼ teaspoon of garlic powder

Cooking Instructions:

1. Set to air-fryer function on 350°F and place the rack in the cooking pot.

2. In a medium bowl, combine all ingredients until smooth and then transfer to a small baking dish.

3. Place the dish on the rack and add the tender-crisp lid and bake for about 30 to 35 minutes or until it is heated through and lightly browned on top.

4. Serve warm immediately.

Caponata

Preparation time: 11 minutes

Cooking time: 30 minutes

Overall time: 41 minutes

Serves: 8 people

Recipe Ingredients:

- ❖ 2 tablespoons of olive oil
- ❖ 1 eggplant, unpeeled & chopped
- ❖ 1 onion, chopped
- ❖ 2 tablespoons of garlic powder
- ❖ ½ cup of pimiento-stuffed green olives, chopped
- ❖ 3 chopped stalks celery
- ❖ 8 ounces of tomato sauce
- ❖ ¼ cup of white vinegar
- ❖ 1/3 cup of brown sugar, packed
- ❖ ¼ teaspoon of hot pepper sauce

Cooking Instructions:

1. Start by setting cooker to sauté on med-high heat and add oil and let it get hot.

2. Once oil is hot, add eggplant, onion, and garlic powder and cook for 5 minutes, stirring occasionally, until eggplant starts to get soft.

3. Stir in remaining ingredients and reduce heat to low. Then cook for 25 minutes, or until all the vegetables are tender.

4. Serve and enjoy.

Mini Steak Kebabs

Preparation time: 16 minutes

Cooking time: 10 minutes

Overall time: 26 minutes

Serves: 12 people

Recipe Ingredients:

- ❖ 1 pound of flank steak (cut in 24 thin slices)
- ❖ ½ cup of peanut butter, reduced fat
- ❖ 2 tablespoons of light soy sauce
- ❖ 2 teaspoons of sesame oil
- ❖ 1 tablespoon of butter
- ❖ 1 teaspoon of red pepper flakes

Cooking Instructions:

1. Soak 24 (6-inch) wood skewers in water for 15 minutes. Then set cooker to air-fryer function on 350°F. Lightly spray the fryer basket with cooking spray.

2. Thread sliced beef on prepared skewers. After that, in a small saucepan over low heat, combine remaining ingredients.

3. Cook while stirring frequently or until butters is melted and sauce is smooth.

4. Place skewers in fryer basket in single layer, these will need to be cooked in batches. Brush sauce over them, making sure to coat them all.

5. Add tender-crisp lid and bake for about 8 to 10 minutes, turning over halfway through cooking time and brushing with sauce again.

6. Repeat with remaining skewers. Once done, serve.

Crispy Sesame Shrimp

Preparation time: 15 minutes

Cooking time: 10 minutes

Overall time: 25 minutes

Serves: 10 people

Recipe Ingredients:

- ❖ 1 cup of flour
- ❖ ¼ teaspoon of salt
- ❖ ¼ teaspoon of cayenne pepper
- ❖ ¾ cup of club soda
- ❖ Nonstick cooking spray
- ❖ 1 pound of peel & devein medium shrimp
- ❖ 2 teaspoons of sesame seeds

Cooking Instructions:

1. In a medium bowl, combine flour, salt, and pepper.

2. Then whisk in club soda until it is thoroughly combined. Spray fryer basket with cooking spray.

3. Dip shrimp, one at a time, in the batter and place in basket in a single layer and sprinkle with sesame seeds.

4. Add tender-crisp lid and set cooker to air-fryer function on 400°F. Cook shrimp for about 8 to 10 minutes or until it turns golden brown.

5. Serve immediately once done.

Cheesy Artichoke Dip

Preparation time: 11 minutes

Cooking time: 15 minutes

Overall time: 26 minutes

Serves: 10 people

Recipe Ingredients:

- ❖ Nonstick cooking spray
- ❖ 2 (13.75) ounces of drain & chop cans artichoke hearts,
- ❖ 4 ounces of diced & drained green chilies
- ❖ 6 tablespoons of mayonnaise
- ❖ 1 ½ cup of grate fine cheddar cheese

Cooking Instructions:

1. Spray a small baking dish with cooking spray.

2. In a medium bowl, combine all ingredients, except ½ cup of cheese and mix well. Spoon into prepared baking dish and top with cheese.

3. Place the rack in the cooker and set the dish on top. Add tender-crisp lid and select air-fryer function on 350°F.

4. Bake for 15 minutes or until hot and bubbly and cheese is nicely browned.

5. Serve warm.

Mini Shrimp Tacos

Preparation time: 20 minutes

Cooking time: 5 minutes

Overall time: 25 minutes

Serves: 8 people

10 Ingredients:

- ❖ Nonstick cooking spray
- ❖ 3 teaspoons of chili powder
- ❖ ¼ teaspoon of salt (divided)
- ❖ 24 medium shrimp, peel, devein & remove tails
- ❖ 1 lime Juice (divided)
- ❖ 1 peeled & chopped avocado,
- ❖ 1/3 cup of sour cream, fat free
- ❖ 1 teaspoon of cumin
- ❖ 2 tablespoons of chopped cilantro, (divided)
- ❖ 24 multigrain tortilla chip scoops

Cooking Instructions:

1. Spray fryer basket with cooking spray.

2. In a large Ziploc bag, combine chili powder and 1/8 teaspoon of salt then add shrimp and toss to coat squarely.

3. Place shrimp, in a single layer, in the fryer basket. Drizzle half the lime juice over shrimp.

4. Add the tender-crisp lid and set to air fryer function on 375°F. Cook shrimp for about 5 to 8 minutes or until they are all pink, stirring halfway through cooking time.

5. In a small bowl, combine avocado and remaining salt and lime juice and mix well.

6. Then in a separate small bowl, whisk together sour cream, cumin, and 1 tablespoon cilantro.

7. To assemble: place 1 teaspoon of avocado mixture and ½ teaspoon of sour cream mixture in each chip. Top with a shrimp and sprinkle of cilantro. Serve immediately

Italian Pita Crisps

Preparation time: 10 minutes

Cooking time: 15 minutes

Overall time: 25 minutes

Serves: 8 people

Recipe Ingredients:

- ❖ 4 (6-inch) whole wheat pita breads
- ❖ 1/3 cup of finely chopped parsley
- ❖ 1 teaspoon of Italian herb seasoning
- ❖ 1/3 cup of finely grated fresh parmesan cheese

Cooking Instructions

1. With a sharp knife, cut away the outside edge of each pita and open the pitas up into 2 halves. Cut each half into 4 wedges.

2. In a small bowl, combine parsley, seasoning, and parmesan. Place pita wedges, in a single layer in the fryer basket, these will need to be cooked in batches.

3. Sprinkle with some of the parmesan mixture. Then add the tender-crisp lid and set to air-fryer function on 350°F.

4. Bake for about 12 to 15 minutes or until golden brown. Repeat with remaining pitas and seasoning.

5. Once done, plate, serve and enjoy.

Mexican Bean Dip

Preparation time: 10 minutes

Cooking time: 10 minutes

Overall time: 20 minutes

Serves: 12 people

Recipe Ingredients:

- ❖ 2 (15 ½) ounces of cans pinto beans (rinsed & drained, divided)
- ❖ 1 cup of salsa, divided
- ❖ 1 teaspoon of olive oil
- ❖ 1 finely chopped onion
- ❖ 1 finely chopped green bell pepper
- ❖ 3 finely chopped cloves garlic
- ❖ 1 tablespoon of coriander
- ❖ 2 teaspoons of cumin
- ❖ ¾ teaspoon of salt
- ❖ ½ cup of grated cheddar cheese,
- ❖ 1 chopped tomato

Cooking Instructions:

1. Add 1 can of beans and ¼ cup salsa to food processor and pulse until smooth.

2. Add oil to the cooker and set to sauté function on medium heat.

3. Once oil is hot, add onion, bell pepper, and garlic and cook for about 5 to 7 minutes or until it becomes tender.

4. Stir in blended bean mixture, remaining can of beans, and seasonings. Bring to a boil, stirring frequently.

5. Reduce heat to low and simmer 5 minutes, stirring frequently. Pour into a serving bowl and top with cheese and tomato. Serve immediately.

White Bean Hummus

Preparation time: 10 minutes

Cooking time: 8 hrs.

Overall time: 8 hrs. 10 minutes

Serves: 8 people

Recipe Ingredients:
- ❖ 2 cups of small white beans, soaked overnight
- ❖ 2 tablespoons of pine nuts
- ❖ 1 teaspoon of grated lemon zest
- ❖ 1 tablespoon of fresh lemon juice
- ❖ ¼ teaspoon of garlic powder
- ❖ ¼ teaspoon of salt

Cooking Instructions:
1. Place beans with just enough water to cover them in the cooking pot.

2. Add the lid and set to slow cooker function on low heat and cook for 8 hours, or until beans are tender.

3. Drain the beans, reserving some of the cooking liquid. Place beans in a food processor.

4. Wipe the cooking pot and set to sauté on low heat. Add the pine nuts and cook, stirring frequently, until lightly browned.

5. Add the lemon zest and juice, garlic powder, and salt to the beans. Pulse until almost smooth.

6. If hummus is too thick, add reserved cooking liquid, a tablespoon at a time, until desired consistency.

7. Transfer hummus to a serving bowl and sprinkle with pine nuts. Serve immediately.

Spicy Black Bean Dip

Preparation time: 10 minutes

Cooking time: 20 minutes

Overall time: 30 minutes

Serves: 12 people

Recipe Ingredients:

- ❖ 2 (16) ounces of rinsed & drained cans black beans (divided)
- ❖ 1 cup of salsa (divided)
- ❖ 1 teaspoon of olive oil
- ❖ ¾ diced fine onion
- ❖ 1 diced fine red bell pepper,
- ❖ 3 diced fine cloves garlic
- ❖ 1 tablespoon of cilantro
- ❖ 2 teaspoons of cumin
- ❖ ¼ teaspoon of salt
- ❖ ¼ cup of grated cheddar cheese reduced fat
- ❖ 1 chopped tomato

Cooking Instructions

1. Add 1 can beans and ¼ cup salsa to a food processor or blender. Pulse until smooth.

2. Set cooker to sauté on medium heat. Add oil and let it get hot. Add the onion, pepper, and garlic and cook, stirring occasionally, 5 to 7 minutes or until vegetables are tender.

3. Add the pureed bean mixture along with remaining ingredients except cheese and tomatoes, mix well.

4. Reduce heat to low and bring to a cook. Let cook 5 minutes, stirring frequently. Transfer dip to serving bowl and top with cheese and tomato. Serve immediately.

Pistachio Stuffed Mushrooms

Preparation time: 5 minutes

Cooking time: 20 minutes

Overall time: 25 minutes

Serves: 8 people

Recipe Ingredients:
- ❖ 16 large mushrooms
- ❖ 1 tablespoon of olive oil
- ❖ ½ finely diced onion,
- ❖ ¼ cup of chopped unsalted pistachios,
- ❖ 1/3 cup of crushed pretzels
- ❖ 2 tablespoons of fat free sour cream
- ❖ 2 tablespoons of chopped fresh parsley
- ❖ ¼ teaspoon of pepper
- ❖ 1/8 tsp hot pepper sauce

Cooking Instructions:

1. Remove stems from mushrooms and dice them. Then set cooker to sauté on medium heat and add oil and let it get hot.

2. Add the chopped mushrooms, onions, and pistachios and cook, until vegetables are tender, about 2 to 4 minutes and transfer to a large bowl.

3. Add the remaining ingredients to the mushroom mixture and mix well. Wipe out the cooking pot and add the rack to it. Select the air-fryer function on 350°F.

4. Stuff the mushroom caps with the filling. Lay a sheet of parchment paper over the top of the rack and place mushrooms on it.

5. Add the tender-crisp lid and bake 20 to 25 minutes or until mushrooms are tender.

6. Preheat oven to 350 degrees F. Remove mushroom stems from caps; finely chop stems. Serve immediately.

Roasted Veggie Dip

Preparation time: 10 minutes

Cooking time: 15 minutes

Overall time: 25 minutes

Serves: 10 people

Recipe Ingredients:

- ❖ Nonstick cooking spray
- ❖ 3 sliced zucchini
- ❖ 1 sliced red bell pepper
- ❖ 1 sliced red onion
- ❖ 2 peeled garlic cloves

Cooking Instructions:

1. Place the rack in the cooking pot and select air-fry function on 400°F.

2. Spray a baking dish with cooking spray and spread vegetables in the pan and spray them with cooking spray.

3. Place on the rack and add the tender-crisp lid and bake for 15 minutes or until vegetables are tender.

4. Then transfer to a food processor or blender and pulse for 30 to 60 seconds or until smooth.

5. Spoon into serving dish and serve warm or cold and enjoy.

Bacon Wrapped Scallops

Preparation time: 30 minutes

Cooking time: 10 minutes

Overall time: 40 minutes

Serves: 8 people

Recipe Ingredients:
- ❖ 1/3 cup of ketchup
- ❖ 2 tablespoons of vinegar
- ❖ 1 tablespoon of brown sugar
- ❖ 1 pound of scallops (rinse & pat dry)
- ❖ Nonstick cooking spray
- ❖ ¼ teaspoon of hot pepper sauce
- ❖ 13 slices turkey bacon, (cut in half)

Cooking Instructions:
1. In a large bowl, whisk together ketchup, vinegar, brown sugar, and hot pepper sauce until it is smooth.

2. Wrap each scallop with a piece of bacon and use a toothpick to secure. Add to the sauce and toss to coat, then cover and refrigerate for 20 minutes.

3. Place the rack in the cooking pot and spray a small baking sheet with cooking spray.

4. Working in batches, place scallops in a single layer on the tray and place on the rack.

5. Add the tender-crisp lid and set to air-fry on 450°F. Cook scallops 4 to 5 minutes, then flip over and cook for another 4 to 5 minutes or until it is cooked through.

6. Serve immediately.

Honey Bourbon Wings

Preparation time: 15 minutes

Cooking time: 11 minutes

Overall time: 26 minutes

Serves: 6 people

Recipe Ingredients:

- ¾ cup of ketchup
- 1 tablespoon of liquid Smoke
- ½ cup of brown sugar
- ¼ cup of finely chopped onion
- 2 finely chopped garlic cloves,
- ½ cup of water
- ¼ cup of bourbon
- 3 tablespoons of honey
- 2 teaspoons of paprika
- ¼ teaspoon of cayenne pepper
- 1 teaspoon of salt
- ½ teaspoon of pepper
- 4 to 5 pounds of chicken wings

Cooking Instructions:

1. Set cooker to sauté on medium heat. Then add ketchup, liquid smoke, brown sugar, onion, and garlic to the cooking pot.

2. Cook while stirring often, until sauce starts to thicken, about 5 minutes. Turn off the cooker.

3. Stir in water, bourbon, honey, and seasonings until it is combined. Add the wings and stir to coat.

4. Secure the lid and set to pressure cooking on high for 5 minutes. When the timer goes off use quick release to remove the lid and line the fryer basket with foil.

5. Transfer the wings to the basket. Set cooker to sauté on medium again and cook sauce until thickened. Pour sauce into a large bowl.

6. Place the basket in the cooking pot and add the tender-crisp lid. Set to air fry on 400°F.

7. Cook wings 6 minutes. Dunk in sauce to coat the wings, then air-fry another 6 minutes. Serve with any remaining sauce for dipping.

South of the Boarder Corn Dip

Preparation time: 5 minutes

Cooking time: 2 hrs.

Overall time: 2 hrs. 5 minutes

Serves: 4 to 8 people

Recipe Ingredients:

- ❖ 33 ounces of corn with chilies
- ❖ 10 ounces of diced tomatoes & green chilies,
- ❖ 8 ounces of cubed cream cheese
- ❖ ½ cup of grated cheddar cheese
- ❖ ¼ cup of chopped green onions
- ❖ ½ teaspoon of diced fine garlic
- ❖ ½ teaspoon of chili powder

Cooking Instructions:

1. Place all ingredients in the cooking pot and stir to mix.

2. Add the lid and set to slow cooking function on low heat, then set timer for 2 hours and stir occasionally.

3. Dip is done when all the cheese is melted and it's bubbly. Stir well and then transfer to serving bowl.

4. Serve warm.

Cheesy Chicken Dip

Preparation time: 11 minutes

Cooking time: 2 hrs.

Overall time: 2 hrs. 11 minutes

Serves: 3 to 6 people

Recipe Ingredients:
- ❖ 1 pound of cubed cheddar cheese
- ❖ 2 cups of cooked & shredded chicken
- ❖ 4 ounces of cubed cream cheese
- ❖ 1 cup of diced tomatoes
- ❖ 1 cup of black beans, drained & rinsed
- ❖ ½ cup of black olives, pitted & sliced
- ❖ 1 seeded & diced jalapeno
- ❖ 2 tablespoons of taco seasoning

Cooking Instructions:
1. Place all ingredients in the cooking pot and stir thoroughly well to mix.

2. After mixing, add the lid and set to slow cooking on low heat. Set timer for 2 hours.

3. Let dip cook, stirring occasionally until hot and bubbly and the cheese has melted.

4. Stir well then transfer to a serving dish and serve warm.

Mexican Rice and Beans

Preparation time: 6 minutes

Cooking time: 3 hrs.

Overall time: 3 hrs. 6 minutes

Serves: 2 to 4 people

Recipe Ingredients:

- ❖ 1 cup of rinsed rice
- ❖ 1 jar salsa
- ❖ 1 can of drained and rinsed black beans
- ❖ 1 packet taco seasoning
- ❖ 1 cup of vegetable broth
- ❖ 2 finely diced garlic cloves
- ❖ 1 seeded and chopped jalapeno,

Cooking Instructions:

1. Place all ingredients in the cooking pot and stir to very mix.

2. Add the lid and select slow cooking on high and then set timer for 3 hours. Cook until rice is tender and dip is heated through and stir well.

3. Once cooking is done, serve immediately.

Jalapeno Meatballs

Preparation time: 11 minutes

Cooking time: 10 minutes

Overall time: 21 minutes

Serves: 4 to 6 people

Recipe Ingredients:

- ❖ 1 pound of lean ground beef
- ❖ ¾ pound of ground pork
- ❖ ½ cup of panko bread crumbs
- ❖ 1 egg, beaten
- ❖ 2 tablespoons of fine diced jalapenos
- ❖ 1¼ teaspoons of cumin
- ❖ 1 grated onion
- ❖ 28 ounces of crushed tomatoes
- ❖ ½ cup of finely chopped fresh cilantro
- ❖ 2 teaspoons of finely diced garlic
- ❖ 1 teaspoon of red pepper flakes
- ❖ ½ teaspoon of cinnamon

Cooking Instructions:

1. In a large bowl, mix together beef, pork, bread crumbs, egg, jalapeno, cumin, and cinnamon, stir thoroughly well then form into meatballs.

2. Add the onion, tomatoes, cilantro, garlic, and red pepper flakes to the cooking pot and place the meatballs in the sauce.

3. Add the lid and select pressure cooking on low and set the timer for 10 minutes. When the timer goes off, use quick release to remove the lid.

4. Transfer meatballs to serving plate and top with sauce. Serve immediately.

Scalloped Potatoes

Preparation time: 11 minutes

Cooking time: 5 minutes

Overall time: 16 minutes

Serves: 6 people

Recipe Ingredients:

- ❖ 5 sliced thin potatoes
- ❖ 5 tablespoons of butter
- ❖ 2 diced fine garlic cloves
- ❖ 1 cup of vegetable broth
- ❖ ¾ teaspoon of salt
- ❖ ½ teaspoon of pepper
- ❖ 1 ½ teaspoons of finely diced fresh parsley
- ❖ ¼ cup of grated cheddar cheese

Cooking Instructions:

1. Place potatoes in the cooking pot and sprinkle with salt, pepper, and parsley, toss to coat.

2. Add butter, garlic, and broth to the potatoes. Add the lid and select pressure cooking on high.

3. Then set timer to 5 minutes; when timer goes off use natural release to remove the lid.

4. Transfer potatoes to serving dish and top with grated cheese to garnish.

5. Serve immediately.

Gingered Butternut Squash

Preparation time: 11 minutes

Cooking time: 15 minutes

Overall time: 26 minutes

Serves: 3 to 6 people

Recipe Ingredients:

- ❖ 8 cups of peeled and seeded butternut squash (cut in 1-inch cubes)
- ❖ 1 cup of water
- ❖ ½ teaspoon of salt
- ❖ 4 tablespoons of butter
- ❖ ¼ cup of half n half
- ❖ 3 tablespoons of honey
- ❖ ½ teaspoons of ginger
- ❖ ¼ teaspoon of cinnamon

Cooking Instructions:

1. Add the squash, water, and salt to the cooking pot and stir thoroughly well.

2. Add the lid and select pressure cooking on high then set timer for 12 minutes. When the timer goes off, use quick release to remove the lid.

3. Drain the squash and place in a large bowl. Add remaining ingredients. Set cooker to saute on medium heat.

4. Cook until butter melts, stirring occasionally. Once the butter melts, pour the sauce over the squash and mash with a potato masher.

5. Serve immediately.

CHAPTER 8 - DESSERTS RECIPES
Buttery Cranberry Cake

Preparation time: 21 minutes

Cooking time: 40 minutes

Overall time: 61 minutes

Serves: 4 to 8 people

Recipe Ingredients:

- ❖ Butter flavored cooking spray
- ❖ 2 eggs
- ❖ 1 cup of sugar
- ❖ 3/8 cup of softened butter
- ❖ ½ teaspoon of vanilla
- ❖ 1 cup of flour
- ❖ 6 ounces of fresh cranberries

Cooking Instructions:

1. Set cooker to bake on 350°F, then spray an 8-inch baking pan with cooking spray.

2. In a large bowl, beat eggs and sugar until light in color and slightly thickened, about 5 to 7 minutes.

3. Add butter and vanilla and continue beating for another 2 minutes. After that, stir in flour just until it is combined then gently fold in cranberries.

4. Spread batter in prepared pan and place in the cooking pot. Add the tender-crisp lid and bake for 35 to 40 minutes or until the cake passes the toothpick test.

5. Remove from cooker and let cool in pan for 10 minutes before transferring to a wire rack to cool completely.

Pumpkin Custard

Preparation time: 11 minutes

Cooking time: 2 hrs. 30 minutes

Overall time: 2 hrs. 41 minutes

Serves: 4 to 6 people

Recipe Ingredients:

- ❖ Butter flavored cooking spray
- ❖ 4 eggs
- ❖ ½ cup of stevia
- ❖ 1 cup of pumpkin puree
- ❖ 1 teaspoon of vanilla
- ❖ ½ cup of sifted almond flour
- ❖ 1 teaspoon of pumpkin pie spice
- ❖ 1/8 teaspoon of salt
- ❖ 4 tablespoons of melted coconut oil

Cooking Instructions:

1. Spray the cooking pot with cooking spray.

2. In a medium bowl, beat eggs until smooth and slightly thickened for about 5 minutes.

3. Gradually beat in Stevia; add pumpkin and vanilla and mix very well. Add the flour, pie spice, and salt and beat to mix thoroughly.

4. Slowly add coconut oil, beating as you do it, and then pour mixture into the cooking pot.

5. Place two paper towels over the top of the cooking pot and add the lid and set to slow cooking on low. Set timer for 2 hours.

6. Cook until custard is done, the center should be set and the sides should begin to pull away from the pot. Serve immediately warm and enjoy.

Gingerbread

Preparation time: 11 minutes

Cooking time: 5 hrs.

Overall time: 5 hrs. 11 minutes

Serves: 6 to 12 people

Recipe Ingredients:
- ❖ Butter flavored cooking spray
- ❖ 1½ cups of self-rising flour
- ❖ ½ cup of flour
- ❖ 1 teaspoon of cinnamon
- ❖ ½ teaspoon of grated fresh ginger
- ❖ ¼ teaspoon of allspice
- ❖ ¼ teaspoon of salt
- ❖ 8 tablespoons of unsalted soft butter,
- ❖ 2/3 cup of light molasses
- ❖ ¾ cup of brown sugar
- ❖ 1 egg, beaten
- ❖ ½ cup of skim milk
- ❖ ½ teaspoon of baking soda

Cooking Instructions:

1. Place the rack in the cooking pot; spray and flour an 8-inch springform pan. In a large bowl, combine both flours, spices, and salt.

2. Place butter, molasses, and brown sugar in a microwave safe bowl. Then microwave on high until butter has melted, mix well to combine.

3. Add butter mixture to dry ingredients and mix well. Whisk in egg until it is thoroughly combined.

4. In a measuring cup or small bowl, whisk together milk and baking soda. Add to batter and mix until blended.

5. Pour into prepared pan and place on the rack. Add the lid and set to slow cooking on high and set timer for 5 hours.

6. Gingerbread is done when it passes the toothpick test. Carefully remove from cooking pot and let cool before cutting and serving.

Chocolate Cake

Preparation time: 15 minutes

Cooking time: 30 minutes

Overall time: 45 minutes

Serves: 16 people

Recipe Ingredients:
- ❖ Butter flavored cooking spray
- ❖ 8 Eggs
- ❖ 1 pound of semi-sweet chocolate chips
- ❖ 1 cup of butter

Cooking Instructions:

1. Place the rack in the cooking pot. Line the bottom of an 8-inch springform pan with parchment paper.

2. Spray with cooking spray and wrap foil around the outside of the pan. In a large bowl, beat eggs until double in size, about 6 to 8 minutes.

3. Place the chocolate chips and butter in a microwave safe bowl. Microwave at 30 second intervals until it is melted and smooth.

4. Fold 1/3 of the eggs into chocolate, folding gently just until eggs are incorporated, then repeat two more times.

5. Pour the batter into the prepared pan and pour 1 ½ cups water into the cooking pot. Place the cake on the rack.

6. Add the tender-crisp lid and set to air fry on 325°F. Bake 25 to 30 minutes or until center is set.

7. Transfer to wire rack to cool. When cool, invert onto serving plate, top with fresh berries if desired. Slice and serve immediately.

Brownie Pie

Preparation time: 16 minutes

Cooking time: 25 minutes

Overall time: 41 minutes

Serves: 12 people

Recipe Ingredients:

- ❖ 2 cups of panko bread crumbs
- ❖ 1 ¼ cup of stevia (divided)
- ❖ ¾ cup of melted, divided butter,
- ❖ 2 teaspoons of vanilla
- ❖ 2 beaten eggs
- ❖ ½ cup of cocoa powder
- ❖ ½ cup of flour
- ❖ ¼ teaspoon of salt
- ❖ 1 cup of chocolate chips

Cooking Instructions:

1. In a medium bowl, combine bread crumbs, ¼ cup Stevia, and ¼ cup melted butter. Press on the bottom and sides of an 8-inch pie plate.

2. In a small saucepan, over low heat, melt remaining ½ cup butter. Stir in remaining Stevia and cook, stirring frequently, until Stevia is dissolved.

3. Remove butter mixture from heat and whisk in vanilla, and eggs until combined.

4. In a small bowl, stir together, cocoa, flour, and salt. Add to butter mixture and stir just until combined. Fold in chocolate chips.

5. Pour brownie mixture into the crust. Place the rack in the cooking pot and place the pie on it.

6. Add the tender-crisp lid and set to air-fry on 350°F. Bake 2 to 25 minutes, and then transfer to a wire rack to cool before serving.

Coconut Lime Snack Cake

Preparation time: 11 minutes

Cooking time: 20 minutes

Overall time: 31 minutes

Serves: 4 to 8 people

Recipe Ingredients:

- ❖ Butter flavored cooking spray
- ❖ 2 eggs
- ❖ ½ cup of coconut milk
- ❖ 3 tablespoons of honey
- ❖ 1 teaspoon of vanilla
- ❖ ¼ cup + 1 tablespoon of fresh lime juice (divided)
- ❖ 1 tablespoon + 1 teaspoon of lime zest (divided)
- ❖ 2 ¼ cups of almond flour sifted
- ❖ 1 teaspoon of baking soda
- ❖ ½ cup of coconut, unsweetened & shredded
- ❖ ½ cup of powdered Stevia

Cooking Instructions:

1. Place the rack in the cooking pot. Spray an 8-inch baking pan with cooking spray.

2. In a large bowl, beat eggs, milk, honey, vanilla, ¼ cup lime juice and tablespoon zest until thick and frothy, about 6 to 8 minutes.

3. Fold in flour, baking soda, and coconut just until combined. Pour into prepared pan.

4. Place the cake on the rack and add the tender-crisp lid. Set to bake on 350°F. Bake 15 to 20 minutes or until cake passes the toothpick test. Let it cool in the pan for 10 minutes, then invert onto a serving plate.

5. In a small bowl, whisk together powdered sugar, remaining tablespoon lime juice, and remaining teaspoon lime zest. Drizzle over the top of cooled cake.

6. Serve immediately.

Almond Cheesecake

Preparation time: 11 minutes

Cooking time: 25 minutes

Overall time: 36 minutes

Serves: 4 to 8 people

Recipe Ingredients:

- ❖ Butter flavored cooking spray
- ❖ 16 ounces cream cheese, fat free, soft
- ❖ ½ cup + 1 tablespoon of sugar
- ❖ 3 eggs
- ❖ 1 teaspoon of almond extract (divided)
- ❖ ½ teaspoon of fresh lemon juice (divided)
- ❖ 1 cup of low-fat sour cream
- ❖ ¼ cup of sliced almonds

Cooking Instructions:

1. Spray an 8-inch springform pan with cooking spray. In a large bowl, beat cream cheese and ½ cup sugar until smooth.

2. Beat in eggs, one at a time. Then add ½ teaspoon almond extract and ¼ teaspoon lemon juice and beat until mixed and pour in prepared pan.

3. Place the pan in the cooking pot and add the tender-crisp lid. Set to bake on 325°F. Bake for 15 minutes, center will still be slightly soft.

4. In a small bowl, combine sour cream, remaining sugar, extract, and lemon juice until smooth.

5. Spread over the top of the cheesecake and sprinkle with almonds. Bake for another 10 minutes.

6. Let cool completely, cover and refrigerate at least 4 hours before serving.

Spiced Poached Pears

Preparation time: 16 minutes

Cooking time: 4 hrs.

Overall time: 4 hrs. 16 minutes

Serves: 2 to 4 people

Recipe Ingredients:

- ❖ 4 peeled ripe pears
- ❖ 2 cups of fresh orange juice
- ❖ ¼ cup of maple syrup
- ❖ 5 cardamom pods
- ❖ 1 cinnamon stick, broke in 2
- ❖ 1-inch peeled & sliced piece ginger

Cooking Instructions:

1. Slice off the bottom of the pears so they stand upright. Carefully remove the core with a paring knife. Stand in the cooking pot.

2. In a small bowl, whisk together orange juice and syrup. Pour over pears and add the spices.

3. Add the lid and set to slow cooking on low. Cook 3 to 4 hours or until pears are soft. Baste the pears every hour or so.

4. Serve garnished with whipped cream and chopped walnuts if you like, or just serve them as they are sprinkled with a little cinnamon.

Caramel Pecan Coffee Cake

Preparation time: 11 minutes

Cooking time: 35 minutes

Overall time: 46 minutes

Serves: 16 people

Recipe Ingredients:

- ❖ Butter flavored cooking spray
- ❖ 3 cups of almond flour, sifted
- ❖ 1 teaspoon of baking powder
- ❖ 1 teaspoon of baking soda
- ❖ ½ teaspoon salt
- ❖ ½ cup of butter, softened
- ❖ ½ cup of Stevia
- ❖ 3 eggs
- ❖ ½ cup of almond milk, unsweetened
- ❖ 1 teaspoon of vanilla
- ❖ ½ cup of caramel sauce, sugar free, divided
- ❖ ½ cup of chopped pecans (divided)

Cooking Instructions:

1. Place the rack in the cooking pot. Spray a Bundt pan with cooking spray.

2. In a medium bowl, combine flour, baking powder, baking soda, and salt, mix well.

3. In a large bowl, beat butter and Stevia until fluffy. Beat in eggs, milk, and vanilla. Stir in dry ingredients just until combined.

4. Pour half the batter in the prepared pan. Top with half the caramel sauce and half the pecans.

5. Use a butter knife to lightly swirl sauce and nuts into the batter. Top with remaining batter.

6. Place the pan and on the rack and add the tender-crisp lid. Set to air fry on 325°F. Bake for 35 to 40 minutes or until coffee cake passes the toothpick test.

7. Let cool in pan 15 minutes, then invert onto serving plate. Drizzle with remaining caramel sauce and sprinkle with remaining nut. Serve immediately.

Peach Cobbler

Preparation time: 15 minutes

Cooking time: 35 minutes

Overall time: 50 minutes

Serves: 4 to 6 people

Recipe Ingredients:

- ❖ Nonstick cooking spray
- ❖ 5 fresh peaches, peeled, pitted & sliced
- ❖ 3 tablespoons of stevia
- ❖ 1 teaspoon of coconut flour
- ❖ ¼ teaspoon of cinnamon
- ❖ 1/8 teaspoon of nutmeg
- ❖ ½ cup of sifted almond flour
- ❖ 1 cup of finely ground oats
- ❖ 1 ½ teaspoon of baking powder
- ❖ ¼ cup of unsweetened almond milk
- ❖ 1 teaspoon of almond extract
- ❖ 2 tablespoons of honey

Cooking Instructions:

1. Place the rack in the cooking pot and spray an 8-inch baking dish with cooking spray.

2. In a large bowl, toss peaches with Stevia, coconut flour, cinnamon, and nutmeg, place in prepared baking dish.

3. In a medium bowl, combine almond flour, oats, baking powder, milk, almond extract, and honey, mix well.

4. Drop by large spoonful over the top of the peaches and place in the cooking pot.

5. Add the tender-crisp lid and set to air-fry on 350°F. Bake for 35 to 40 minutes until top is lightly browned. Serve warm immediately.

Banana Cinnamon Snack Cake

Preparation time: 11 minutes

Cooking time: 25 minutes

Overall time: 36 minutes

Serves: 4 to 6 people

Recipe Ingredients:
- ❖ Butter flavored cooking spray
- ❖ 1 ½ cup of flour
- ❖ ½ cup of sugar
- ❖ 2 teaspoons of baking powder
- ❖ 1 teaspoon of baking soda
- ❖ 2 teaspoons of cinnamon
- ❖ ½ teaspoon of salt
- ❖ 1 cup of vanilla yogurt, low fat
- ❖ 2 mashed bananas
- ❖ 2 tablespoons of melted coconut oil
- ❖ 1 egg
- ❖ 1 teaspoon of vanilla

Cooking Instructions:
1. Place the rack in the cooking pot. Spray an 8-inch baking dish with cooking spray.

2. In a large bowl, combine dry ingredients and mix very well. Add remaining ingredients and mix until it is combined, then pour into prepared dish and place on rack.

3. Add the tender-crisp lid and set to bake on 400° and bake for about 20 to 25 minutes or until golden brown and the cake passes the toothpick test.

4. Cool in pan for 10 minutes, then invert onto serving plate and cool completely. Serve and enjoy.

Steamed Lemon Pudding

Preparation time: 16 minutes

Cooking time: 90 minutes

Overall time: 1 hr. 56 minutes

Serves: 4 to 6 people

Recipe Ingredients:

- ❖ Nonstick cooking spray
- ❖ ¾ cup of butter, unsalted, soft
- ❖ 1 teaspoon of baking powder
- ❖ Zest & juice from 2 lemons
- ❖ 1 cup of caster sugar
- ❖ 2 eggs
- ❖ 2 cups of flour

Cooking Instructions

1. Lightly spray a 1-liter oven-safe bowl with cooking spray; then add the butter and sugar to the bowl and beat until it becomes light and fluffy.

2. Add the eggs, one at a time, beating well after each addition. Then stir in the flour and baking powder until it is thoroughly combined.

3. Fold in the lemon zest and juice and mix until its smooth, then cover it lightly with foil.

4. Pour 1 ½ cups of water into the cooking pot and add steamer rack. Place the bowl on the rack and secure the lid.

5. Set to steam on 212°F and cook for 90 minutes or until pudding is cooked through.

6. Remove the pudding from the cooker and let it sit for 5 minutes before inverting onto serving plate.

Pumpkin Crème Brulee

Preparation time: 11 minutes

Cooking time: 3 hrs.

Overall time: 3 hrs. 11 minutes

Serves: 4 people

Recipe Ingredients:

- ❖ 1 egg yolk
- ❖ 1 lightly beaten egg
- ❖ ¾ cup of heavy cream
- ❖ 4 tablespoons of pumpkin puree
- ❖ 1 teaspoon of vanilla
- ❖ 4 tablespoons of sugar (divided)
- ❖ ¾ teaspoon of pumpkin pie spice

Cooking Instructions:

1. Whisk together egg yolk and beaten egg in a medium bowl and mix thoroughly well.

2. Again, whisk in cream, slowly until it is fully combined. Stir in pumpkin and vanilla and mix until combined as well.

3. In a small bowl, stir together 2 tablespoons sugar and pie spice. Add to pumpkin mixture and stir to blend.

4. Fill 4 small ramekins with mixture and place in the cooking pot. Carefully pour water around the ramekins; it should reach halfway up the sides.

5. Add the lid and set to slow cooking on low. Then cook for 2 to 3 hours or until custard is set.

6. Sprinkle remaining 2 tablespoons over the top of the custards and add the tender-crisp lid and set to broil on 450°F.

7. Cook for another 2 to 3 minutes or until sugar caramelizes, be careful not to let it burn and transfer ramekins to wire rack to cool before serving. Serve immediately and enjoy.

Mexican Chocolate Walnut Cake

Preparation time: 11 minutes

Cooking time: 2 hrs. 30 minutes

Overall time: 2 hrs. 41 minutes

Serves: 4 to 8 people

Recipe Ingredients:

- ❖ ½ cup of cocoa powder, unsweetened
- ❖ 2 teaspoons of baking powder
- ❖ Butter flavored cooking spray
- ❖ 1½ cups of flour
- ❖ 2 teaspoons of ground cinnamon
- ❖ ¼ teaspoon of cayenne pepper
- ❖ 2 cups of grated zucchini
- ❖ ¾ cup of chopped walnuts (divided)
- ❖ 1/8 teaspoon of salt
- ❖ 1 cup of sugar
- ❖ 3 beaten eggs,
- ❖ ¾ cup of coconut oil melted
- ❖ 2 teaspoons of vanilla

Cooking Instructions:

1. Spray the cooking pot with cooking spray and line the bottom with parchment paper.

2. In a medium bowl, combine dry ingredients and mix very well. Then in a large bowl, beat sugar and eggs until it becomes creamy.

3. Stir in oil, vanilla, zucchini, and ½ cup walnuts until combined. Fold in dry ingredients just until it's combined.

4. Pour batter into cooking pot and sprinkle remaining nuts over the top. Add the lid and set to slow cooking on high.

5. Cook for 2 ½ hours or until cake passes the toothpick test. Then transfer cake to a wire rack to cool before serving. Serve once cool and enjoy.

Date Orange Cheescake

Preparation time: 21 minutes

Cooking time: 20 minutes

Overall time: 41 minutes

Serves: 4 to 8 people

Recipe Ingredients:

- ❖ Butter flavored cooking spray
- ❖ 2 cups of water
- ❖ 2 pound of ricotta cheese
- ❖ 4 eggs
- ❖ ¼ cup of sugar
- ❖ ¼ cup of honey
- ❖ ½ orange zest Juice f
- ❖ ¼ teaspoon of vanilla
- ❖ 1 cup of finely chopped dates (soak in warm water 20 minutes)

Cooking Instructions:

1. Place the trivet in the cooking pot and add 2 cups of water and spray a deep, 8-inch spring form pan with cooking spray.

2. In a large bowl, beat ricotta cheese until it becomes smooth. In a medium bowl, beat eggs and sugar for 3 minutes then fold into ricotta cheese.

3. In a small saucepan, heat honey over low heat, do not let it get hot, just warm.

4. Whisk in orange juice, zest, and vanilla until it is thoroughly combined. Whisk into cheese mixture until combined. After that, fold in dates and pour into prepared pan.

5. Cover with foil and place the cheesecake in the cooking pot and secure the lid. Set to pressure cooking on high then set the timer for 20 minutes.

6. When timer goes off use natural release to remove the lid. Transfer cheesecake to wire rack to cool completely. Cover and refrigerate at least 4 hours before serving.

7. Once done, serve and enjoy.

Steamed Blackberry Pudding

Preparation time: 11 minutes

Cooking time: 50 minutes

Overall time: 61 minutes

Serves: 4 to 6 people

Recipe Ingredients:

- ❖ Butter flavored cooking spray
- ❖ 1 ½ cups of water
- ❖ 5 ¼ tablespoons of soft butter
- ❖ 8 tablespoons of caster sugar
- ❖ 1 lemon zest
- ❖ 2 eggs
- ❖ 1 cup of flour
- ❖ 4 tablespoons of milk
- ❖ 4 tablespoons of honey
- ❖ 1 ½ cups of blackberries

Cooking Instructions:

1. Start by spraying 6 ramekins with cooking spray, then pour the water in the cooking pot and add the steamer rack.

2. In a large bowl, beat butter, sugar, and lemon zest until it becomes light and fluffy.

3. Beat in eggs, flour, and milk until combined and stir in 2 tablespoons of honey.

4. Drizzle the remaining honey in the bottoms of the ramekins. Add blackberries and pour the pudding mixture over them.

5. Tent the ramekins with foil, leave some space for puddings to rise while cooking. Place the ramekins on the steamer rack.

6. Add the lid and select steam function and cook for 40 to 50 minutes, or until puddings pass the toothpick test, then transfer to wire rack to cool slightly.

7. To serve, invert onto serving plates and top with whipped cream if desired, or just eat them plain. Serve and enjoy.

Coconut Cream Dessert Bars

Preparation time: 6 minutes

Cooking time: 2 hrs.

Overall time: 2 hrs. 6 minutes

Serves: 5 to 10 people

Recipe Ingredients:

- ❖ Butter flavored cooking spray
- ❖ 1 cup of heavy cream
- ❖ ¾ cup of powdered Stevia
- ❖ 4 eggs
- ❖ ½ cup of coconut milk, full fat
- ❖ ¼ cup of melted butter
- ❖ 1 cup of unsweetened and grated coconut
- ❖ 3 tablespoons of coconut flour
- ❖ ½ teaspoon of baking powder
- ❖ ½ teaspoon of vanilla
- ❖ ½ teaspoon of salt

Cooking Instructions:

1. Start by spraying the cooking pot with cooking spray. Then place cream, Stevia, and coconut milk in a food processor or blender. Pulse until it is thoroughly combined.

2. Add remaining ingredients and pulse until combined and pour mixture into cooking pot.

3. Place two paper towels over the top and add the lid and set to slow cooking on high.

4. Now cook for about 1 to 3 hours or until center is set. Carefully remove lid so no moisture gets on the bars.

5. Transfer cooking pot to a wire rack and let it cool for 30 minutes. Refrigerate, uncovered at least 1 hour. Now Cut into 10 squares or bars and serve immediately.

Strawberry Cheescake

Preparation time: 6 minutes

Cooking time: 8 hrs. 20 minutes

Overall time: 8 hrs. 26 minutes

Serves: 4 to 6 people

Recipe Ingredients:
- ❖ Butter flavored cooking spray
- ❖ 16 ounces of soft cream cheese
- ❖ 2/3 cup of powdered Stevia
- ❖ 1 teaspoon of vanilla
- ❖ 2 eggs on room temperature
- ❖ 1 cup of chopped strawberries

Cooking Instructions:

1. Place the trivet in the cooking pot and add enough water to cover bottom by 1 inch, then spray an 8-inch spring form pan with cooking spray.

2. In a large bowl, beat cream cheese until smooth and beat in Stevia and vanilla until combined. Beat in eggs, one at a time and beat until it is thoroughly combined.

3. Then pour into prepared pan and cover bottom and sides of pan with foil to prevent any water from leaking in. Place the pan on the trivet.

4. Add the lid and select pressure cooking on high and then set timer for 20 minutes.

5. When the timer goes off, use natural release to remove the lid. Transfer cheesecake to wire rack to cool completely.

6. Cover and refrigerate 8 hours or overnight. Top with chopped strawberries before serving.

7. Serve immediately done and enjoy.

Sweet Potato Pie

Preparation time: 6 minutes

Cooking time: 45 minutes

Overall time: 51 minutes

Serves: 10 people

Recipe Ingredients:
- ❖ Butter flavored cooking spray
- ❖ 4 baked & cooled sweet potatoes
- ❖ ½ cup of skim milk
- ❖ 1 tablespoon of sugar free maple syrup,
- ❖ ½ cup of brown sugar
- ❖ 2 eggs
- ❖ 1 tablespoons of butter, soft
- ❖ 1 teaspoon of cinnamon
- ❖ 1 teaspoon of vanilla

Cooking Instructions:
1. Place the rack in the cooking pot. Spray an 8-inch pie plate with cooking spray.

2. Scoop out the flesh of the potatoes and place in a large bowl.

3. Add remaining ingredients and beat until smooth and pour into pie plate and place on the rack.

4. Add the tender-crisp lid and set to bake on 400°F. Bake for 40 to 45 minutes or until a knife inserted in center comes out clean.

5. Transfer pie to a wire rack to cool and cover and refrigerate until ready to serve.

6. Serve immediately once ready.

Citrus Steamed Pudding

Preparation time: 11 minutes

Cooking time: 1 hr.

Overall time: 1 hr. 11 minutes

Serves: 4 to 8 people

Recipe Ingredients:

- ❖ 3 tablespoons + 1 teaspoon of soft butter
- ❖ Butter flavored cooking spray
- ❖ 3 ½ cups of water (divided)
- ❖ 1 cup of sugar (divided)
- ❖ 2 cups of sifted self-rising flour
- ❖ 1 peel & pith removed chopped orange,
- ❖ 1 ½ tablespoons of cornstarch
- ❖ 2 teaspoons of finely grated orange zest
- ❖ 1 tablespoon + 2 teaspoons of finely grated lemon zest
- ❖ 2 eggs
- ❖ ¼ cup of milk
- ❖ ¼ cup + 1 tablespoon of unsweetened and divided orange juice

Cooking Instructions:

1. Spray a 6-cup oven-safe bowl with cooking spray and pour 2 cups of water in the cooking pot and add the steamer rack.

2. In a large bowl, beat 3 tablespoons of butter, ½ cup of sugar, and 4 teaspoons of orange and lemon zest until it becomes smooth.

3. Beat in eggs, one at a time, and beating well after each addition. In a small bowl, stir together milk and ¼ cup orange juice.

4. Fold flour, orange pieces, and milk mixture into butter mixture, alternating between ingredients, begin and end with flour.

5. Pour into prepared bowl and tent with foil and tie with kitchen string and place on the steamer rack.

6. Add the lid and set to steam and cook for 1 hour or until the pudding passes the toothpick test then transfer to wire rack.

7. Drain any remaining water from the cooking pot and set cooker to saute on medium heat.

8. Add remaining sugar and cornstarch to the pot. Slowly pour in 1 ½ cups water, stirring constantly until combined. Cook for 5 minutes, or until its thickened.

9. Stir in tablespoon of lemon juice, tablespoon orange juice, tablespoon lemon zest, and teaspoon butter and cook until butter has melted and mixture is smooth.

10. To serve: invert pudding onto serving plate and drizzle sauce over the top.

11. Slice and serve immediately.

Irish Cream Flan

Preparation time: 16 minutes

Cooking time: 10 minutes

Overall time: 26 minutes

Serves: 3 people

Recipe Ingredients:

- ❖ ¼ cup + 2 tablespoons of sugar (divided)
- ❖ 1 tablespoon of water
- ❖ 1 cup of half and half
- ❖ ¼ cup of Irish cream flavored coffee creamer
- ❖ ¼ cup of Irish cream liqueur
- ❖ 2 eggs

Cooking Instructions:

1. In a small saucepan over medium heat, heat ¼ cup sugar until it is melted and a deep amber color. Swirl the pan occasionally to distribute the heat.

2. When the sugar reaches the right color remove from heat and carefully stir in the water until combined.

3. Drizzle over the bottoms of 3 ramekins. Then in a small oven-safe bowl, whisk the eggs.

4. In a small saucepan over medium heat, stir together half and half, creamer, Irish cream, and remaining sugar and heat to simmering.

5. Gradually whisk the warm liquids into the eggs, 2 tablespoons at a time, whisking constantly.

6. After a 1/3 of the cream mixture has been added, slowly pour the remaining mixture into the eggs, whisking constantly until it thoroughly combined.

7. Pour 1 cup water into the cooking pot and add the trivet. Pour the egg mixture into the ramekins and cover tightly with foil.

8. Place them on the trivet. Secure the lid and set to pressure cooking on high. Set the timer for 5 minutes.

9. When the timer goes off, use natural release to remove the lid and then transfer custards to a wire rack and uncover to cool.

10. Cover with plastic wrap and refrigerate at a total period of 4 hours before serving.

11. Use a small knife to loosen the custards from the sides of the ramekin and invert onto serving plate.

12. Serve immediately and enjoy your meal.

Portuguese Honey Cake

Preparation time: 15 minutes

Cooking time: 15 minutes

Overall time: 30 minutes

Serves: 4 to 8 people

Recipe Ingredients:

- ❖ Butter flavored cooking spray
- ❖ 3 egg yolks on room temperature
- ❖ ¼ cup of honey
- ❖ 4 ½ tablespoons of cake flour
- ❖ 2 eggs, room temperature
- ❖ 2 tablespoons of powdered sugar

Cooking Instructions

1. Place the rack in the cooking pot and spray an 8-inch round baking dish with cooking spray and lightly coat with flour.

2. In a large bowl, beat egg yolks, eggs, and powdered sugar until combined.

3. In a small saucepan over medium heat, heat honey until it starts to simmer. Let it cook for 2 minutes.

4. With mixer running, slowly beat in the hot honey. Beat mixture for about 8 to 10 minutes or until it turns pale and thick and doubled in size.

5. Gently tap the bowl on the counter to remove any air bubbles. Sift flour into mixture and gently fold in to combine.

6. Pour the batter into the pan and tap again to remove air bubbles and place the cake on the rack.

7. Add the tender-crisp lid and set to bake on 350°F. Bake the cake for 15 minutes, center should still be soft.

8. Transfer to a wire rack and let cool in pan 30 minutes. Invert onto serving plate and serve immediately.

Blackberry Crisp

Preparation time: 21 minutes

Cooking time: 45 minutes

Overall time: 66 minutes

Serves: 6 people

Recipe Ingredients:

- ❖ 6 cups of blackberries
- ❖ 2 tablespoons of sugar (divided)
- ❖ 1 tablespoon of cornstarch
- ❖ 1 cup of oats
- ❖ ½ cup of almond flour
- ❖ ½ cup of chopped almonds,
- ❖ 1 teaspoon of cinnamon
- ❖ ¼ teaspoon of salt
- ❖ ¼ cup of melted coconut oil

Cooking Instructions:

1. Add the rack to the cooking pot and spray an 8-inch baking dish with cooking spray.

2. In a large bowl, add the blackberries, 1 tablespoon sugar, and cornstarch, toss to coat, then pour into prepared dish.

3. In the same bowl, combine oats, flour, nuts, cinnamon, salt, coconut oil, and remaining sugar, mix well and pour over berries.

4. Place the dish on the rack and add the tender-crisp lid and set to bake on 350°F.

5. Bake for about 30 to 35 minutes or until top is golden brown and transfer to wire rack to cool before serving.

6. Serve immediately.

Acknowledgement

In preparing the "Healthy Ninja Foodi Cookbook for Beginners", I sincerely wish to acknowledge my indebtedness to my husband for his support and the wholehearted cooperation and vast experience of my two colleagues - Mrs. Emily Cook and Mrs. Alexander Peterson.

Barbara Cutts